DEFENDING MY LIFE

SURVIVING A BULLY'S TORTURE

C. MICHAEL SMITH

Defending My Life: Surviving a Bully's Torture
by C. Michael Smith

Copyright © 2012 Christopher M. Smith

Published by Earnest Publishing House LLC, Merrifield, Virginia

Perfectbound ISBN   978-0-9858301-2-0
eBook ISBN 978-0-9858301-3-7

"Long is the way, and hard, that out of hell leads up to light."

—John Milton

Acknowledgements

I am forever grateful to the following people for their contributions in my life and to this project:

To my wife, Julie, thank you for being the "light at the end of the tunnel" for me and also the voice of reason in my sometimes turbulent life. We've endured a mountain of chaos together. I could not imagine a better partner with whom to share all the days of my life. My love for you grows every day and has no end.

To my mom and dad, I will never be able to properly thank you for all that you've contributed to my life in the past and present. You've stuck by me through it all and exemplify what every parent should strive to achieve. I love you with all of my heart.

To my daughter, Ashlyn, you've been very brave and strong in spite of all the challenges you've faced. You will always be my little angel and I am grateful to have you in my life. Let us strive to improve our relationship together every year as you continue to grow from being my little girl into the woman of whom I am so proud.

To Julio and Victoria, you epitomize everything that is great in a parent. You picked Julie and I up when we were down and have made it possible for us to survive in spite of almost insurmountable odds. You've provided us with an endless line of support and these few words do not express my never-ending gratitude.

To bookcovers.com, thank you for making the book design and publishing process so simple for me. You have been easy to work with and have supplied me with tremendous value for all the work you've done on this project of mine.

Preface

In the past, strategies for dealing with a bully have varied. They may have included keeping a safe distance to avoid getting hurt, standing up to the bully, or falling victim to the bully's demands, threats, or torment. Of course these ideas or variations of them continue to exist today because sometimes that bully is inescapable. Depending on the situation, the results of the bullying may include physical harm and/or mental anguish that can even lead to suicides and death in the most extreme of cases.

Fortunately schools and other organizations have begun to acknowledge the unhealthy consequences of bullying and are implementing aggressive methods to address this mounting problem. Let's put an end to bullying through the education of our children, family, teachers and staff through community workshops and policies of zero-tolerance for this type of behavior. Let us intervene to stop any incident of bullying. There is no justification for bullying in any situation. It is simply about taking unfair advantage of someone by dominating, intimidating, or simply victimizing a fellow human being.

According to some leading sources on anti-bullying:

- 13 million kids will be bullied in the United States this year.
- 1 out of every 4 kids is bullied.

- 80% of the time, an argument with a bully will end up in a physical fight.
- 1/3 of students surveyed said they heard another student threaten to kill someone.
- Playground statistics - Every 7 minutes a child is bullied. Adult intervention 4%. Peer intervention 11%. No intervention - 85%.
- 160,000 students stay home from school everyday due to bullying.
- 25% of kids being cyber bullied don't tell anyone about it.
- 9 out of 10 LGBT (lesbian, gay, bisexual, and transgender) students have been bullied while at school.
- 282,000 students are physically attacked in secondary schools each month.
- Approximately half of all teens have experienced some form of cyber bullying.
- In schools where there are anti-bullying programs in place, bullying is reduced by 50%.

This book recounts my struggle as a victim of another's bullying. The story is based entirely on true events. The names, places and some minor details have been changed to protect people's identities, however the events are recounted as I experienced them.

I do not advocate the use/consumption or abuse of alcohol by minors or anyone. Please remember that consumption of any type of beverages containing alcohol by minors is dangerous, unhealthy, and against the law. Do not drink if you are under the age starting from which the applicable laws allow you to drink.

One

Looking back, I realize just how much I feared Dickie Hellerman on the morning I shot and killed him out in the backwoods of my parents' property.

Even though Dickie and I went to the same high school, we were from hugely different circumstances and had little in common. Still at 16 years old, five feet tall, barely tipping 100 pounds, with an innocent face and a disposition to match, I was not the kind to make enemies. If I had any, I was unaware of them. I came from a modest family who had raised me on old-fashioned values. I was a quiet kid in my junior year who detested the kind of trouble that seemed to follow Dickie wherever he went.

Dickie weighed nearly two hundred pounds and was a lot taller than I was. He was a senior on the varsity football team and was a year ahead of me. He was a kid who frequently drank to excess, usually growing violent and looking to kick someone's butt whenever he did.

Although I felt awkward about my simple background and family circumstances, I had been successful in using my personality in a bid for class president that year. Like all the candidates, I was asked to stand up in front of the entire class and give a speech on why my classmates should vote for me. Lacking any other good reason why I should be elected, I decided to offer up a number of thoroughly unachievable campaign promises. I figured it just might get a laugh from my friends and classmates too. My list included selling cigarettes and chewing tobacco at our afternoon refreshment breaks, giving mandatory days off for juniors, installing doors on all of the bathroom stalls, installing soda dispensers in the cafeteria, right down to making sure there were salt and pepper shakers on every lunch table.

My speech had incited a minor riot that day in the cafeteria. My friends were all in attendance and whistling loudly at every outlandish item I announced. There were cheers and whistles and hoots in general from all my classmates. By the end of the speech, I had everyone standing up on their chairs. I concluded by pointing my finger into the crowd and proclaiming,

"I, and only I, can make these policies happen. So if you want to have a great junior year, you'd better vote for me, Justin Bailey!"

I headed back to my seat to high-fives and a standing ovation. Suddenly, I was a rock star. When the votes were counted, I had won in a landslide.

In addition to being class president in my junior year, I was on the wrestling team and was a member of the drama club. I especially enjoyed being involved with the latter. Our class staged a number of performances in the school auditorium, our version of a *Saturday Night Live* skit being one of the most memorable evenings for me. It was called *The Coneheads' Family Feud* and I was the host of the show.

This happened to be one of the first moments when I crossed paths with Dickie and yet I doubt either one of us gave it much thought as things were unfolding. He was up in the front row snapping pictures with his camera. I was busy trying to steal the show.

I don't know that Dickie had particularly noticed my existence until the time an old classmate of ours, Randy, threw a big party at his house. Randy's parents had gone out of town for the weekend. It was a perfect opportunity for some fun so he and his gang pooled their money to buy a couple of cases of beer. It was a chilly spring evening and most of the kids had stayed inside Randy's house. He managed to keep those who spilled outside in the backyard. As this wasn't exactly a sanctioned event, Randy was doing his best not to annoy the neighbors.

I happened to be in the living room talking with friends when we heard something like a 4-wheeler racing outside.

"What the heck?" Randy yelled and pulled back the window curtains. "Damn it!" he shouted and let the curtain drop. "It's Dickie Hellerman! He's out there on my parents' lawn on a 4-wheeler."

Randy started pacing around, frantically trying to figure out what his next move would be.

"Oh man! What am I going to do now?"

While Randy paced and fretted, people took their turn peeking out through the curtains. Dickie was making a lot of noise. When I looked out, I noticed bits of shrubs and flowers had gotten stuck in the grill of Dickie's 4-wheeler. It looked like he had cut through a number of yards on his way out to Randy's place. He had definitely broken a few traffic laws. We were way out in the country, so he had to travel a long distance to get out there, and that 4-wheeler surely wasn't licensed to operate anywhere on normal streets.

With news of Dickie's presence quickly spreading through the party, people were beginning to realize the party mood was changing.

"Damn it! Here we go again," was the general sentiment.

Some people were looking for their car keys. Dickie was sure to pick a fight, and if you stuck around long enough, it might just be with you. The only thing preventing people from leaving was that Dickie's 4-wheel exhibition out on the lawn had created a scene. It was like a train wreck that you couldn't stop watching.

After what seemed like forever, Dickie finally parked and dismounted from his 4-wheeler. He was staggering like the party had begun for him a long time ago. By that time, everyone was crowded into the living room. The cautious window checks continued. Taking my turn, I saw Dickie poking around inside a large ice chest strapped to the back of his ride. Out came a bottle of beer. Down went a long chug.

"Wow," I said. "He practically guzzled the whole beer."

Randy poked his head out next to mine.

"Get this," he whispered. "That whole ice chest is filled with beer."

"Yeah, he must be planning a long night of it."

Hoping to salvage what remained of his party, Randy gathered several of his buddies and went to confront Dickie. Not wanting to get into an altercation with him, they made sure to keep their distance.

"Dude, look what you did to my parents' lawn," Randy said.

Dickie belched, smiled and had another slug.

"Come on, bro," Randy said diplomatically. "You're gonna have to go, okay?"

"I don't gotta go anywhere…BRO!" Dickie replied sarcastically.

He got on top of his 4-wheeler, kicked back and drank some more.

"Okay, he's not leaving!" Randy said to his girlfriend. "Call the cops."

With that, Dickie got off of his 4-wheeler and came after Randy.

"That's messed up, man," Randy said, backing his way into the house. The front door was quickly closed. Randy pushed through the crowd that had gathered around the windows and peered outside.

"What's he doing?" someone asked.

"He's not leaving, that's for sure!"

"Are you kidding me? someone asked.

"Yep," Randy said.

"He just cracked open another bottle of beer."

"Did you call the cops?" Randy called out to his girlfriend.

She came into the room, looking stressed out.

"Yeah, I called them," she said.

"Are they coming?"

"Yeah, but they said it might take half an hour to get here."

Things inside settled down a bit, but people were still wondering if Dickie would make some kind of move. I took another look outside at one point and Dickie turned my way. I quickly dropped the curtain again.

By the time the cops pulled up, Dickie was back to prowling around on the lawn looking for someone to hassle. He had the bottle of beer in his hand and was swearing at the house, the moon, and anything that happened to grab his attention.

Seeing the cops arrive, he immediately took a defensive position.

"Come on, Dickie," one of the cops said cautiously. "You're going to have come with us now."

"I ain't goin' nowhere," Dickie screamed back.

"Come on, Dickie, you're in no condition to drive anywhere with that 4-wheeler."

The cops started to circle Dickie and he moved with them, apparently assessing his options. To everyone's surprise, and startling the two cops in particular, Dickie charged at them. As they went down from Dickie's tackle, the other cop jumped on top and tried to gain control. What went down at that point can best be described as a wild scuffle, with Dickie punching and kicking and the two cops struggling to get handcuffs on him.

When they finally succeeded in getting Dickie face down, one cop put a knee in his back and the other wrestled with the cuffs. Dickie was screaming and struggling the whole time.

"Screw you! I'll kill you! I'll kill you! I'm not going anywhere!"

When at last Dickie was being escorted to the police cruiser, he looked over at the house and I just happened to be looking out the window at that moment.

"What are you looking at, Justin?" he shouted and spat in my direction. "Come on out here, you little pussy! Come on! Next time I see you, I'm going to kick your ass!"

Great, I thought, and dropped the curtain. Now every time I saw Dickie around school, I'd have to worry about getting pummeled. There'd be no peace until he graduated in June. Thank God he was a senior. It was the only consolation I could draw from this situation.

Hearing more commotion, I looked back outside and saw the cops hustling Dickie over toward the police cruiser. The door was open but Dickie quickly jumped up and got both his feet up against the frame. The same wild battle that had played out on the lawn was being repeated in midair. When Dickie was finally secured in back, the cops slammed the door shut and fell against the car in relief.

All things considered, they had been fairly diplomatic up to that point. We lived in a small town in the middle of nowhere. Everybody knew everybody and the cops were well acquainted with Dickie's family. However, when Dickie got himself turned around inside the cruiser and attempted to kick the glass out of the back window, he had pushed them too far.

One of the cops went for the trunk. The other cop yelled in at Dickie.

"Knock it off, Dickie, it's only gonna get worse for you."

The threat failing, they soon had Dickie back out on the front lawn, face down, his mouth full of grass and the whole struggle began again.

Once Dickie had been suited up with a set of leg irons and was reasonably subdued in the back of the cruiser, Randy opened the front door and the party tentatively trickled out onto the front lawn again. One of the cops was keeping an eye on Dickie. The other one was on the phone to the station, asking dispatch to see if she could get in touch with Dickie's father.

There was a lull of a minute or so before dispatch came back on the line.

"I talked with Mrs. Hellerman. Basically Roy has been tying one on himself."

"Well, did you talk to Roy yourself?"

"Yeah, he got on the phone with her for a minute. He said, 'Oh goddamn it, not again.' "

"So, what's he going to do about Dickie?"

"Well, given his condition, I told Roy he'd better stay out of his car."

"All right. 10-4. We'll be back at the station shortly."

The cop finished with dispatch and looked at his partner.

"Damn, what a night!"

"Yeah, so what else is new?"

"All right. Let's get this idiot down to the station and we'll deal with the old man later on."

The lead cop came over, had a look inside the house, gave

us the "behave yourselves" lecture and climbed back into his cruiser. We watched as they headed off down the road. The party resumed for the most part although we were all dumfounded by the outrageous displays we had just witnessed. Really, who fights with cops like that?

I worried about seeing Dickie at school but he was nowhere to be seen. He wasn't seen the next day, or the next one, or the next.

It wasn't until later on that a copy of Dickie's arrest report made its way around school. The story spread like wildfire and was shocking in its detail.

According to the report, once the police got Dickie to the precinct, they offered him a deal. He had been to a rehab facility called Shady Brook Lodge a few months earlier. If he would check himself back in for a tune-up, they'd drop the charges. Dickie refused and the police report contained a verbatim account of his response: Dickie had a gun at home. He slept with it. He was fond of sticking it into his mouth and ultimately had plans of using it to kill off the entire Hellerman clan, including himself.

Taking into account Dickie's drunken state, the cops decided it best to leave the cuffs and leg irons on until the old man arrived to pick him up. Dickie's father did finally hitch a ride some time later, still plenty loaded himself, and a candidate in his own right for driving under the influence. However, being a big contributor to the local police force, Roy was handed a cup of coffee and was told to sober up.

As drinkers went, Roy had been a reasonably successful one. He was a business owner and made a pretty decent living, but he drank habitually and lived his life as habitual drinkers usually do. There was a full-service bar off the living room at his home, with beer and every imaginable kind of booze.

Back at the police station, when it appeared that Dickie had sufficiently sobered up, the cops removed his cuffs and leg irons. All hell broke loose. Released from his shackles, Dickie went after his father. The cops muscled Dickie onto the floor and got him back into handcuffs, only to discover Dickie's father flat on the linoleum floor behind them, having a heart attack.

While an ambulance carted the old man away on a stretcher, Dickie resumed the chatter about shooting himself and the whole goddamned family. He was going ballistic. His old man may have had one foot in the grave, but that was the last thing on his mind.

With Roy in the hospital, the cops sent Dickie off to be examined at the nearest mental hospital. A refresher course back at Shady Brook Lodge followed. The buzz about this episode continued around school but finally died down after a few days.

Some students felt badly for Dickie, some were glad to see him take a hit. But no one doubted he drank too much, and that bad things always followed when he did.

Dickie was gone from school for a month or so and in his absence I started dating Maria again. She may have broken up with me to be with Dickie but I didn't care. I was head over heels for her and that's all that mattered to me.

Two

Some months before that episode at Randy's place, Dickie had also managed to crash a party at my house. I don't really think Dickie's initial intention was ever to ruin everyone's fun, but once you put booze in him, that was usually the result. Dickie showed up and things quickly dissolved from there.

My parents had gone away for the weekend and the preparations began. There was a bar nearby and that was where we always bought our beer as kids in high school. The bar was a real dive too. The old guy who owned it was called Skeeter Johnson. He was as redneck as you could possibly get for my neighborhood.

The one time I had gone along for the beer run, I was thrown off by his general appearance. Skeeter had a lip full of chewing tobacco and was spitting into an empty beer can. His oily hair was disheveled and from his looks, I imagined personal hygiene was not a priority for him.

Given that I was the youngest looking, my friends usually had me wait out in the car. In the case of my party, two of my buddies went in and made the buy. I could see Skeeter glancing in every direction as he took their money. When they came out a few minutes later, they walked around to the back of the bar. That was the way Skeeter liked things. A lot of his customers were shady, just like he was, but Skeeter didn't want anyone getting wind of his suspect deals.

That moment of arriving back at my house with the beer was one of terrific excitement for all of us. This was going to be a fantastic night or so I thought.

None of us seemed to care that we drank the cheapest beer we could find. As long as it gave us a buzz we would have our fun. My buddies and I each cracked open a beer at that point and got things ready for the party.

Darkness settled in. It was a late fall evening and for weeks autumn leaves had been falling to the ground around my house. The night air was pungent with the scent of dying leaves.

I had closed my parents' house and told everyone to stay out of it. The last thing I needed was for my folks to come home and find their place trashed. I started a big bonfire out in my parents' back yard halfway to my father's hunting cabin. We had a sizable area between the house and the cabin where we could party. Kids started arriving and the party revved up. A lot of people did land inside the hunting cabin and just as many stayed in the yard by the bonfire.

As the evening wore on, I completely lost control of the situation in the main house. Apparently some girls had gone in to use the bathroom, and then, they just naturally continued to visit there. Others had joined them and soon the place was overflowing with bodies. Yielding to peer pressure and reluctant to spoil the fun, I tried to manage things as best I could without running everyone off.

Over time a number of people got drunk, and with kids coming and going from my parents' house, I was starting to panic.

I was outside when Troy came by and told me that someone had thrown up in the cabin. I went in to investigate and found the entire place had been trashed. There were empty beer cans everywhere. After cleaning up the vomit, I went to check on the main house and freaked out. It was like a scene out of *Animal House.*

As I attempted to get things back under control, the door to my parents' bedroom opened and a girl named Crystal came staggering out. A guy from the football team came out with her. She was drunk and he had a big stupid grin on his face. Crystal grabbed the next guy she could get her hands on and dragged him into the bedroom. The door closed. The first guy went around the living room high-fiving his friends.

"What the heck?" I said to my friend Donnie. "What's going on?"

"I think that Crystal is trying to bang everyone on the football team."

"Are you kidding me? In my parents' bedroom?"

Donnie shrugged. Everyone was chuckling like it was big fun.

"I can't believe what a tramp Crystal is being," I muttered.

As I headed back outside, a bolt of anxiety shot through me. What if my parents came home early? I had to get this mess cleaned up or my parents would freak out.

I went in and tried damage control in the hunting cabin first. My friends were still partying around me.

All of a sudden, my buddy Ted came in and proclaimed,

"Hey Dickie just showed up."

Ted was about Dickie's size.

"You have got to be kidding me," I said, pacing around with my hands in my hair. "How did he find out about the party?"

Dickie had come uninvited and had to go out of his way to get there. My folks owned forty-two acres, a couple of miles down Quarry Road. Our modest little house was two hundred yards up a steep gravel lane through the woods. Then another hundred yards from that road on our driveway. If one car was heading up the hill and someone else was coming down, it was a real adventure just inching around each other.

"Well, with half the football team here, I guess it was inevitable that he would find out."

I stood there for a moment trying to figure some convenient way to get rid of him.

"What's he doing?" I asked.

"Nothing yet. He came with Zach. They're all smiles so far."

"Oh man, the two of them are always getting into fistfights."

Ted shrugged.

"Can you keep an eye out for me please? I'm trying to clean up this mess a little."

"Will do, buddy."

"Thanks dude."

Ted headed back outside. I went back to cleaning up. Worries about Dickie and the possibility that my folks may come home early consumed my thoughts. Having Dickie appear was the very last thing I needed right now.

Shortly afterward, Ted was back.

"Hey, Dickie and Zach are going at it out in your driveway."

"Oh man! Over what?"

"Absolute nothing. Zach said something about the football team losing to Springfield every year."

"Well, ain't that the truth?"

"Hey, screw you, dude. I'm on the football team, too."

"But still, how stupid is that? The jerk is always going off over something completely trivial. It doesn't take much to get Dickie going does it?"

That was Dickie, just add liquor and he was like a grenade without its pin. One wrong word and watch out.

"Come on, Ted. You've got to help me get him out of here."

Ted came along reluctantly. Like me, he was not a violent person. Two other guys came with us. I found Dickie and Zach in the driveway, pummeling each other with reckless abandon. It took a couple of guys from the football team to pry them apart. Dickie's sister Rhonda was there crying and screaming and trying to get Dickie into their car.

"Come on, Dickie. Let's just go," she said over and over again.

Dickie pushed her away.

"I'm gonna kick his ass!" he said.

Zach already had a couple of bruises from his scuffle with Dickie.

"Look everyone has got to leave now," I said with Ted and Troy beside me.

"Who do you think you are, Justin?" Dickie said.

Dickie came at me, but Ted and Troy got between us.

"This is his house," Troy said.

Dickie looked startled at first. But eventually resorted to his normal drunken antics.

"Oh, he lives here," Dickie said mockingly.

"Come on, Dickie," his sister begged, pulling on his arm again.

"All right, the heck with them. The fun's over at this party anyway."

Dickie got into the car with his sister like he was doing everyone a favor. They drove off. I turned to find almost everyone else heading out also.

"Hey guys, I'm really sorry," I said.

"It's not your fault, Justin," somebody said as they went by.

One more time, Dickie had wrecked the fun. What a bummer. Truth be told, I was glad it was over. Having Dickie around made me nervous.

Exhausted, I collapsed in the living room. The place was still a mess. I was awakened early the next morning to the sound of a car pulling up the driveway. I jumped to my feet in a panic. I had a massive hangover and my head was splitting.

Oh no, what if it's my parents? I glanced outside and saw that it was. I was trying to come up with convenient excuses as they walked in the front door. My mother stopped in her tracks, heartbroken. My father was furious.

"What the hell happened here, Justin?"

My father poked his head into their bedroom.

"Goddamn it!" he said. "Come look at this!"

I approached sheepishly. Apparently Crystal had vomited in my parents' bed while she was banging one of the football players.

My father took a tour of the property, unloading on me the entire time. The backyard and cabin were a total disaster. My mother didn't say much, but I could see the disappointment on her face.

"We're going to Grammy's house for a few hours," my dad said. "When we get back, this mess had better be gone!"

I spent those next few hours throwing out trash, cleaning and trying to bring the house and cabin back to normalcy. When my folks got back home, my father grounded me. That meant hard labor in the woods and around the house for an unspecified time.

I went to school on Monday, dreading what I expected to be a run-in with Dickie. Oddly, he didn't mention a thing about Saturday night. He ignored me like he had no idea where he had been.

I guess in a way that exchange characterized the way I had always felt in relation to Dickie -- not very important. I doubt I was alone in those feelings. I mean, how could anyone ever really know him? One minute he was Dr. Jekyll, the next minute, Mr. Hyde.

A few days later, I was helping my mother in the kitchen when my father arrived home from work. He worked as a correctional officer and had on that grim-looking gray uniform they all wore, with a cap to match. He wasn't a particularly tall man, but stocky and definitely nobody to mess with. I always felt a bit intimidated by him when he walked in the door, especially since that episode with the party.

My father still wasn't talking to me. My mother was cooking dinner and he kissed her. They exchanged greetings. My father hung his hat and headed off to clean up.

"Dad?" I asked nervously.

He stopped.

"What?"

"It's Drama Night at school this Friday."

"And?"

"Well, I can't go if I'm still grounded."

He looked at my mother.

"It's an important part of his school curriculum," she said.

That wasn't exactly true, but like the wonderful person she was, my mom was always trying to back me up.

"Sounds like goofing off to me. What's it about?" he said to me.

"A bunch of cool stuff, Dad. One of the plays is called the *Conehead Family Feud*. It's an old *Saturday Night Live* skit."

"Oh, for Christ's sake."

He looked at my mother.

"I play Bill Murray's character, the host of the show."

"And you call that education?"

"It's an official school function, babe. People are counting on him to be there."

My father went off still grumbling but eventually gave me the okay. My parents came along to watch that night despite my dad's frustration.

That night the drama club did several one-act plays, with *The*

Conehead Family Feud being our grand finale. As I mentioned before, I played the host of the show. Bill Simpson played the father Conehead. Bill and I had known each other since we were in junior high school together. In those years we were both members of the wrestling team. Now Bill was 6' 4", about 290 pounds, and played on the football team. He was good friends with Dickie.

The night of the play, I started checking the auditorium a good half hour before the performance got off the ground. The house was packed with family and friends. The sight of all those familiar faces had me very nervous. When the curtain went up on the first skit, there was Dickie in the front row, snapping pictures like a paparazzo.

In the end, all of the plays went beautifully and we received several curtain calls. Each of us had our names read, each bringing another round of applause. I had been the lead in two of the plays and received a standing ovation as did several others. Mom and Dad were clapping and whistling from their seats. I was overjoyed that they were so excited for me. The whole time this was going on, Dickie was down in front, hamming it up like he had been the star of the show.

In front of the school, I heard the kids talking about a party at a classmate's house. She had a big house in a very affluent neighborhood called Sutton View. Bill came by and asked if I was going.

"Please," I said to my father.

"It's your call," he said to my mother.

"It's part of being a kid and growing up, honey."

He wasn't that happy about it, but gave her a nod.

"You go ahead," she said to me. "But please be home by midnight. And if you can't get a ride, call me and I'll come get you."

"Okay, Mom. Goodbye, I love you."

"We love you, too."

"Oh, and thanks, Mom and Dad."

"Just be careful."

My friends and I ran off in our excitement. Everyone who had been in the plays showed up at the party including a bunch of other people I was friends with.

Just as the party was getting into full swing, Dickie showed up. Shortly afterward, a fight had started and I went outside to see what the commotion was all about. Predictably the fight was over nothing special and Dickie was involved. A couple of guys were holding him back. The host was really upset and asked everyone to leave before the cops came.

Donnie gave me a ride home. Another evening turned sour.

"He is always starting a fight," I said.

It was an old line. It was an old story.

"Dickie could be a good guy," Donnie said. "He just gets so crazy when he drinks."

"And he always seems to be drinking, so when is he a good guy?"

Donnie and I laughed, then drove in silence.

"By the way, Justin, you were great tonight," he said when he dropped me off.

"Thanks," I said, and gave him a thumbs up.

"By the way, are you still grounded?"

"Yeah, unfortunately."

"Okay, I guess I'll pick you up for school on Monday morning."

"Yeah, thanks," I said again, and closed the door.

Donnie almost always gave me a ride to school. After I spent a long, boring weekend of chopping wood and doing errands around the house, Donnie showed up Monday in his red '84

Subaru wagon. We headed off to school on a two-lane road, winding this way and that through the steep back mountain.

Donnie had Led Zeppelin's "Heartbreaker" blasting away. We were lost in our own little world, jamming to the music, and not much aware of anything else. All of a sudden Dickie appeared alongside us in his beat-up dingy black 1980 Malibu wagon, He was doing about ninety and passing us in the other lane. Seeing it was two of his classmates, Dickie slowed down long enough to make funny faces and flip us the bird.

Entertained by his own antics, Dickie failed to notice oncoming traffic. Donnie and I started pointing frantically but Dickie was too busy making faces, unaware that his life was about to end. Only at the last minute did he take notice and swerve to avoid a head-on collision, then he barreled off. The last we saw of him, he was weaving in and out of traffic as we got nearer to school. When we saw him at school that day, not a word was said. Dickie acted as if the near-death experience had never occurred.

That was Dickie, I guess -- in his best moments, the crazy guy, clowning around and throwing caution to the wind; at his worst moments, drunk and looking to make someone's life difficult. He was still legally a boy, but whenever he drank, the boyishness completely left him. If you saw him coming and could tell that he'd been drinking, you disappeared or suffered the consequences. In both cases, Dickie always leaped before he looked and didn't give much thought to where he was landing.

Three

It's hard to say whether or not girls were into me during my first few years of high school. It's possible, but not the way that I had wished. They considered me cute, like some kind of teddy bear.

"Justin, you're such a cute little guy," they frequently told me.

My sophomore yearbook was filled with such sentiments. I suppose with my size and basically shy demeanor, I came off as harmless to them -- which I was happy to do, as long as that view of me could still translate into actual romance. I had been trying for a couple of years to move in that direction, without any success. It seemed that girls had classified me as the buddy type and that was all I meant to them.

The day I first saw Maria was magical to me, though. It was at one of our high school football games. The team was called the Black Stallions. Our school colors were black and grey. The team was pretty good that year. With little else to do in town, the games were a major destination for a lot of folks.

One saturday as Donnie and I walked across the student parking lot to get to the game, we passed the tailgate party that the Hellermans held at every home game. They put on a full spread, too: grilled hot dogs and burgers and tons of ice-cold beer from what I saw. The odd thing was that they were the only family to host a tailgate party at a high school football game.

Not that I had given much thought to the situation. My mind was pretty much focused on getting together with my friends, looking for girls and that particular day at the game was no exception. My friends and I were like nomads all throughout the game, sometimes up in the bleachers, sometimes walking around and cracking jokes. We had hardly paid any attention to the games, in any case.

I am at a loss to say whether our team won or lost that day. Odds are they won, but either way I've forgotten most of the details, except for the moment when I first locked eyes with Maria. She smiled and the warmth in her pretty, chestnut-brown eyes immediately touched me. She was barely five foot tall and gorgeous.

Donnie was going crazy about Sean Walters banging out some serious yardage down on the field, but I was oblivious. Maria had given me a look in passing and all of my attention was focused on her.

Seeing me distracted, Donnie started shaking my arm.

"Dude, are you listening to me or what?"

I wasn't. Maria was still staring back over her shoulder at me. Those beautiful brown eyes had swept me away.

As my buddies headed off in the other direction, talking about what they planned to do after the game, I was lost looking back at Maria, wondering who she was and where she went to school and why I had never seen her before. As she disappeared into the crowd, a sense of loss came over me. What if I never saw her again? What if I had just let the opportunity of a lifetime slip through my fingers?

Later on that evening, I ran into my buddy Ted. He was a lineman on the football team.

"What's the matter, buddy? You look kind of down."

I told him about the girl I had seen.

After hearing my description, Ted said,

"Hey, I'm pretty sure I know the girl you're describing. Her name's Maria. She's a friend of mine and lives right around the corner from me."

"No way!" I said. "Oh man. You've got to introduce me."

"Sure, I'll call her the first chance I get."

"Okay, but don't say it's about me, I'd be way too embarrassed. Just tell her you're stopping by to chill out for a while and I'll just happen to tag along."

Ted went off to get something to drink and I went off walking on a cloud.

The following morning, my father and I went out to the woods to gather some firewood. It was a chore my brothers and I had been helping my father do since we were little kids. Each fall, my father went through the forest cutting down enough wood to get us through the cold season. The fallen logs had a chance to dry out over the next few months and then he went back to cut them into manageable lengths. That morning my father drove his rusty old stick shift Dodge Ram truck as close as possible to our work, and from there we had to make repeated trips, hand-carrying and throwing the shorter logs back to the truck.

"You can go on home and clean up, Justin," my dad said when we were nearly done that afternoon. "I'll finish up here and walk home. Tell your mom I'll be back in just a bit."

I took the loaded truck home and spent a good hour splitting and stacking the firewood alongside the house.

After a shower, I did some homework upstairs, then helped my mother with dinner. The time was growing late. Darkness was settling in over the woods. Mom was beginning to get worried about my father.

"Maybe you'd better go back and check on him with the truck," she said.

I had the truck door open when my father came crashing out from the woods in a great rush.

"Let's get inside the house. Come on, quickly! Come on, come on!" he barked when I failed to satisfy his sense of urgency.

"What's the matter, Dad?" I asked, as he had a last look around before closing the door.

He went into the kitchen without answering and I followed.

"What on earth is wrong?" my mother asked.

Dad sat down at the kitchen table and slumped over, all out of breath.

"You won't believe this but some wild dogs cornered me on the way back home."

"Oh my God!" Mom exclaimed.

"Isn't that crazy? Fortunately I was near my tree stand. I got up there and watched for over an hour while they circled around below."

Mom came over and leaned on my father's back, hugging him.

"My goodness, babe, you could have been bitten or even killed."

"Yeah, I was preparing to stick it out for the night, but they must have gotten wind of something else because they finally went loping off in the woods. I gave it a good fifteen minutes to make sure and hauled ass back here as fast as I could."

Mom came around so my father could see her.

"Honey, there are bears and God knows what else, out there in the woods. You need to start carrying a gun with you whenever you're out there, all right?"

My mother looked at me.

"You too, Sugarbear. I don't want either of you out there

unprotected from now on. Promise you'll take one of the rifles along with you, okay?"

As an avid deer hunter, my father owned several rifles. He rarely took them out, unless he was hunting.

"Look, honey," my dad said. "I understand your concern, but a rifle is a bit impractical. You leave it in the truck and the next thing you know you've got a bear or these wild dogs between you and the gun."

"I don't care," she persisted. "I'll feel a lot less worried if you have it anywhere nearby. Now promise me please."

"Look, I have a better idea. I'll go buy a handgun tomorrow. That way we can have a little holster and keep it on us at all times."

"Well, whatever you say, honey, but I'm not letting you back out there until you're properly armed."

They kissed.

"I love you, babe. I'll drive down into town in the morning. Justin can do his homework until I get back. Now let's say we have some of that world-famous spaghetti and meatballs of yours. I'm famished after all that running for my life."

He smiled and winked. She smiled back through her concern.

"You go clean up and I'll get things on the table."

My father was gone in the morning when I woke up. I heard him return a little before noon. I closed my books and went downstairs. He walked in with a box and opened it on the kitchen table. It was an old-looking pistol. My father showed it to my mother and me.

"It's a .22 caliber."

"You think that's powerful enough?" Mom said.

"Oh, sure. No need to go ballistic."

"Ha ha," she said.

"Here, see what you think," my father said to me.

I held it.

"Wow, this is the first time I've ever held a pistol."

"Well, what do you say we have some lunch and we'll get a bit of target practice in before we go get another load of firewood?"

"Cool" I said.

My mother made us something to eat and afterward, she cleaned up while my father and I took the .22 out to his makeshift target range. It was a bale of hay with a target tacked to it about a hundred yards from the front of the house. A hill rose behind the bale of hay so we never worried about any stray shots going into the woods and accidently hurting someone.

My father loaded the pistol and proceeded to give me a lecture on gun safety. Keep the safety on until you're ready to shoot. Make sure everyone is behind you. It was the same stuff I had heard every time my brothers and me were shown how to use a rifle.

My father fired off a few rounds.

"You see, a .22 caliber is small enough so you don't get a big kick when it goes off, but it's deadly enough to kill a wild dog at close range."

He fired it a few more times and handed it to me. I took several shots.

"Okay, that's good enough."

He slipped it into its holster and strapped to his waste.

"Now let's go gather up another load of firewood."

We drove back and forth several times that afternoon, gathering wood in the forest, unloading it, and splitting and stacking the wood next to our house.

Late in the afternoon, Ted pulled up in the driveway. My father said hello and went inside for a drink. I leaned up against the firewood and set my dad's big homemade maul down next to me. The stack of wood was over twenty feet long and eight feet tall. There was a rock wall behind the wood and an overhang above to keep it dry.

"What's up, Ted?" I asked.

"It's a done deal, buddy."

"What do you mean?"

"The meeting with Maria. Did you forget about her already?"

"No. Are you kidding me?"

I was beside myself with excitement.

"That is so cool," I said.

"Yeah I know. I told you I'd take care of it for you. She told me to stop by on Monday evening after school."

"But you didn't tell her about me, did you?"

"No. It's cool. I said something like, 'I haven't seen you in ages,' and she said, 'I know, why don't you stop by on Monday and we'll play some pool.' So we'll just show up together like you said."

"Oh man," I said. "I'm really freaking out here."

Thinking of actually meeting Maria face to face, I was unable to sit still. That Ted knew her was some consolation, but not much. He may have looked the part of a hunk -- 6' 4", 275 lbs, handsome and a real bruiser, on both the wrestling and football teams, but he had never had sex either and was just as awkward around girls as me.

"So, are you cool?" he asked.

"Yeah, yeah. I'm cool," I giggled.

My father came back out and put on his gloves.

"So, Ted, you guys beat the crap out of Summit last weekend. Nice job."

"Thanks, Mr. Bailey. Anyway, I gotta get home for dinner, so I'll see you on Monday," Ted said.

"Yeah, I'll see you on Monday, Ted."

odbye, Mr. Bailey."

"Take it easy, Ted," Dad answered.

Dad and I went back to work, splitting wood. He would set up a log. Then I'd give it a whack and we'd stacked the pieces up in the growing pile. Over and over the process went, with my mind totally lost on Maria now.

On Monday evening, I went to Ted's house and we walked over to Maria's place on foot. Ted knocked on her door as I stood behind him. She answered with a big smile and gave Ted a hug. He introduced me as one of his friends. She said "hi" and invited us in. I had no idea what to say and was tripping over my words. Noticing that my hands had grown sweaty, I started to freak out. Maria was even prettier than I had remembered. Every time I looked into those big brown eyes, my heart beat heavily. I was trying to think of cool things to say, but the more I tried, the more I felt my chest tightening.

Inside, Maria asked if we wanted anything to drink, then took us on a tour of the house for my benefit. There were four floors, four bedrooms, a library, a full bar and a heated pool. Her parents even had a Jacuzzi in their master suite. The basement was very cool with all kinds of video games and pinball machines. It had a really nice view of Hardey's Lake from the living room and made my parents' house look tiny in comparison.

The tour done, Maria invited us down to the basement to play some pool. Ted racked up the balls. I stood there, shifting my feet and trying not to look awkward. When I glanced at Maria, she smiled.

"I think I saw you at the game last Friday."

"Oh yeah!" I said. "I think I remember seeing you, too."

She smiled like she knew I was pulling her leg and didn't care. We sipped on our drinks. Ted had finished racking up the balls.

"Okay," he said. "Who wants to break?"

Being a horrible pool player, I now had something new to freak me out. Maria figured to be a hotshot player, what with a pool table in her own house. I decided my best shot was to be a gentleman and gestured for Maria to go first. She did. Her cue stick glanced off the cue ball and it barely made a dent in the rack. I repressed a laugh, but Maria was quickly laughing at herself and Ted chimed in.

I invited Ted to go next and he also muffed his shot. I didn't do much better and pretty soon the three of us were joking about what lousy pool players we were.

The whole time, I kept stealing glances at Maria. She was just so cute and I kept imagining my arms around her. When I said something witty and Maria laughed, I felt on top of the world. I was ecstatic that I seemed to be making progress with her.

When it was time to leave, Maria escorted us to the front door.

"Hey, it was good to see you," Ted said, and gave her a hug.

"It was really cool meeting you," I said.

Maria shook my hand. I stood there, trying to find the courage to ask her out.

"Hey, could I have your number?" I blurted out as she started to close the door. She reopened it. "I mean, I'd really like to see you again."

"Like go out on a date or something?" she asked.

"Yeah, yeah. Maybe I could buy you dinner and take you to a movie or something like that."

"Sure, that sounds great," she said.

She went off and came back with her number written down on a piece of paper. There was a heart drawn around her number.

"Sweet," I said, trying not to look too excited. "I'll talk to you soon."

I walked down to meet Ted and we left. As soon as we were around the first bend in the road, I let out a loud "Yes!"

"Unbelievable, man! I can't believe I did it and it's all thanks to you, Ted."

Ted gave me a high-five.

"I was not going to rest tonight if I didn't ask her."

I pumped a fist and let out a big sigh of relief.

"Now I'm really not going to get any sleep tonight."

And I hardly did sleep. In the wee hours of the morning, I was still up, thinking of Maria and how good it felt to have been that close to her. I finally dozed off with her phone number lying next to my pillow.

Figuring it was best not to appear overly eager, I waited a few days before giving her a call. Besides having to arrange a date, I had to arrange for the use of my folks' car. Around our place you earned privileges by working for them. Go chop some wood, make sure your chores are all done, then you can use the car. It wasn't exactly boot camp, but when it came to my dad, I always had to do something to get something, in this case the use of the car.

If only the reward had been something better. To say that my folks' car was basic was an understatement. I squirmed at the thought of pulling up in Maria's driveway in it. But I managed to put those thoughts aside at the thought of being with her.

I had also been obsessing about what to wear on our first date. I wanted to look extra cool. When I had come downstairs with my third outfit on, my dad joked, "Third time's a charm."

"Ha, ha. Real funny, Dad."

"You look nice," my mom said.

"Don't be too late, okay?" my dad said, as I headed out the door.

"Sure. See you later. I love you guys."

"We love you, too."

On the way over to Maria's house, I tried to think of clever things to say. I was extremely self-conscious and paranoid about what others thought and I worried endlessly about the car. There were absolutely no extras or power anything on this car. Even the radio dial was manual.

I arrived and rang the doorbell, nervous as hell. Maria's mother answered with a big smile.

"Come on in, Justin. I'm Ellen. Maria is still getting ready."

I followed Ellen into the living room. Maria's father and her little brother and sister were watching a movie.

"This is my husband, Nick, and her little brother and sister, Joey and Janie."

Nick stood up and reached out to shake my hand. It was like grabbing a handful of bananas. I was surprised by his appearance. With the big, splashy house on the lake, I had expected a business executive type. Instead, he looked more like a regular dude with his tinted, wire-framed glasses. He was a big man, well over six feet and heavyset, with his hair done in a comb-over. The hair kind of looked like it had been dyed with black shoe polish. He was wearing a black sweatshirt, faded blue jeans and white high-top sneakers.

"Hey, Justin," he said. "Come sit down and join us. We're watching *Back to the Future*. It's hilarious."

I walked over, but nervously remained standing. The kids turned to look at me once and went back to the movie.

"You have a really nice house," I said to Nick.

"Yeah, yeah, thanks" he said without looking.

"I love this movie," I said.

He nodded, again without looking.

A moment later I felt a tap on my shoulder.

"All ready? We should probably get going."

I turned to view Maria in a beautiful dress. She looked amazing.

"Wow, you look great!"

"Thank you," Maria said.

She went over and gave her mom and dad a kiss.

"Now take care of my daughter, Justin," Nick said half jokingly as we headed out the door.

"I will, sir."

Outside, I nervously thought of what I would say next as I opened her car door like a gentleman. Maria smiled as she got in and that put me as ease a little.

"Where are we going tonight?" she asked when I got behind the wheel.

"I thought we could get something at Joe's Pizza, then go see a movie. What do you think?"

"That sounds great."

That was more relief. Joe's was right around the corner on Hardey's Lake, so less time for me to sweat over something brilliant to say.

We sat across from each other at the pizza place and fumbled through a conversation while we waited for our server. Everything between us was filled with anticipation and heart flutters. I felt sweat beading up under my shirt.

When the waitress came, we ordered a salad to go with our pizza. Then I was back to feeling anxiety again.

"So," I said. "I can't believe that we've gone to school together for all this time and we're just getting to know each other now."

"I was thinking the same thing. How could we have missed each other at such a small school?"

"So you never noticed me at all," I said.

She laughed.

"So you never noticed me."

"Well, I'm a junior and you're a senior so maybe that's it."

Our food came and we started to eat.

"Ted tells me that you're both on the wrestling team. Maybe I can come see you wrestle sometime."

"That would be great. Our team is really awesome."

"I suck," I added jokingly.

Maria laughed and I was in heaven to think she was so interested in me.

When we finished eating, I paid for the meal and we headed back out to the car. The movie house was in town, about twenty minutes away. I was still hung up about trying to think of stuff to talk about.

"So, how do you like Mr. Lucas for English class?" she asked me.

"I think he's pretty cool. What about you?"

"Yeah, me too. I think he's okay. Are you taking Spanish or French?"

"Spanish."

"Me too!"

We spoke a bit in Spanish and laughed at ourselves. She started to tell me about her family and somehow most of my anxieties slipped away.

The movie theatre was swarming when we got there. We stopped outside to look at the movie posters.

"I love scary movies," Maria said. "Can we see *Child's Play*?"

"Sure, whatever you want." I was just relieved that she had picked one. I had even been in a panic about doing that right, too.

The movie stunk but I eventually got up the courage to reach over and grab hold of Maria's hand. She squeezed back like we had been doing it for years. I sat there enthralled.

After the movie, we made our way out to the car, holding hands. As I opened the car door for her, she stopped and looked into my eyes. My heart was fluttering again. The kiss I wanted so badly was so close and yet seemed so far away. I didn't know how to get it.

"That was some awful movie, huh?" she said.

"I thought it would never end."

She giggled. I got lost in the melodic sound of her laugh.

While we were stood staring at each other, I awkwardly lurched out to kiss her. Maria responded warmly. I held her a moment longer.

"So that's what it's like," I said when we were done.

"Are you telling me you've never kissed someone before?"

"Oh, don't you worry," I said. "I've kissed plenty."

She smiled like she didn't believe me, but I wasn't about to tell her the truth.

On our way back to her place, everything was relaxed between us. One kiss had made me feel comfortable with Maria. She reached across and held my hand. I smiled and she smiled back. We drove along listening to music and mostly thinking our own thoughts.

At her place, I opened her door and she exited. I was expecting to leave but she asked me to come inside for a while.

We went into the living room.

"Why don't you pick out a movie for us to watch? I have to let my folks know I'm home. Let's make it better than the last one."

"No pressure or anything," I said.

She laughed and started to leave.

"Hey," I said, looking around in confusion, "where are they?"

"Oh, sorry. All the movies are in the library. Come on, follow me."

She led me from the kitchen to the library. I was stunned but didn't say it. There must have been over a hundred movies to choose from.

"I'll see you in a minute," she said.

I was still looking when Maria came back.

"So what did you pick?"

"There are so many, I can't make up my mind."

I closed my eyes and pointed.

"That one."

Maria laughed.

"You want to watch *Pretty in Pink*?"

"I meant to pick out *Top Gun*."

"Sure," she said.

She grabbed *Top Gun* to bail me out and we went back to the living room. I really didn't care what movie it was. I was just thrilled to be there.

Maria put the movie in and sat tight against me on the couch. I had never been happier in my whole life. The movie started. Our hands touched. I was staring at the TV but my mind was not the least bit focused on it. Eventually, Maria leaned over to kiss me again and we held each other close.

All during this time I had heard her parents moving around upstairs. Then suddenly her father was in the kitchen.

"Justin, you want a sandwich? I'm having one." Nick said.

I could tell he was checking on us. He had made sure to speak very loudly with his hand on the open refrigerator door.

"No, thank you, sir," I said. "I really have to get going."

Maria and I stared at each other and I got up to leave. She followed me out through the kitchen.

"Take care, Mr. Gallo."

"Sure I can't fix you a sandwich or something?"

"No, I'm fine, thanks."

Outside the door, we shared one more lingering kiss.

"Call me when you get home, okay?"

"Okay," I said.

I drove home with my mind in a fog, possibly in love for the first time in my life and with the moments of our evening playing over and over in my head.

Four

The following day at school, I ran into Maria at lunch and she invited me back over to her house that afternoon. I told Donnie I had something else to do and met Maria at her car when school ended. She had a 1985 white Thunderbird with black interior. I got in, surrounded by leather and her perfume and girly scents. It was a really cool ride and one more reminder of the simple background I came from.

When we arrived at Maria's house, she grabbed us a couple of drinks and invited me to play pool in the basement again. I racked up the balls and let her take the first shot. She laughed at her terrible break.

"So, tell me about your family," I said while I lined up my first shot.

"Well there's not much to tell, really. You met my younger brother and sister -- they're in elementary school. I also have an older sister. She's in her early twenties and is a huge Grateful Dead fan."

"Where is she right now?"

"She and her boyfriend are out there following the Grateful Dead on a world tour right now."

"Wow, cool." I said, not really knowing what that meant.

"Yeah, she should be back sometime soon. My parents are in

sales so they spend most of their time out on the road. The kids take the bus home from school and won't be home for a while."

I missed a bank shot and stood up.

"Your shot."

As Maria lined up her shot, her body brushed against mine. I set the pool cue down and we started to kiss.

"Let's go up to my room," she said, after a minute.

Lying down on her bed, we held each other tightly. We kissed passionately and caressed each other with tenderness.

"God, you have a great body," I panted "and you smell really good too."

Maria breathed heavily.

We continued to explore our newly discovered passion and I was beside myself with excitement.

Afterward, we had lain there for some time gazing at each other when I happened to notice a photo of this guy named Greg up on Maria's bookshelf. Then I noticed another one of them over on her desk.

"What, are you like going out with Greg or something?"

"No, we broke up. Well, he broke up with me."

"Well it sort of looks like you're still hung up on him or something."

"No. Well, maybe. I don't know."

She went into a long soliloquy about their relationship, how Greg did this and Greg did that. On and on she went, in particular about how he had dumped her, but she was okay now. She didn't care. I felt really second-rate all of a sudden. I had come to hate this Greg guy thoroughly without even knowing him.

"Anyway, I haven't seen him in over a month," Maria concluded.

I lay there, staring at the ceiling.

"What?" she asked.

"Let's just not talk about it, okay?" I said.

"Okay, that's fine," she said and snuggled up to me.

I looked up at the pictures of Greg and Maria staring down at me. The two of them seemed so happy and I felt pretty dumb about trying to fill his shoes. It was my first time in love. I was unaware that it could quickly lead to so much heartache and uncertainty.

The next day at school I went about my normal routine.

Maria came up to me at lunch.

"Where have you been? I've been looking for you all day."

"Oh, just busy I guess."

"You're still sore about Greg, aren't you?"

"Well, I can't get over all the Greg memorabilia you have in your room."

"I'm sorry about that."

I was unconvinced and still a little agitated. She tried tickling me.

"I want to come by and see your place after school, okay?"

I thought of saying no. I was still mad, but also embarrassed to show Maria our dumpy little house in the woods. We didn't even have cable television or air-conditioning. I was especially worried because my mother had started a load of laundry that morning before I left for school and that meant she could have clothes strung out from one end of the living room to the other when I got home. We had a washing machine, but no dryer, so in the fall and winter when it was damp outside, the laundry got strung out to dry from a rope in front of the wood burner in the living room.

"Okay?" Maria asked, shaking me from my thoughts.

"Yeah, okay," I said.

She laughed.

"You're so cute."

I spent the rest of the day being annoyed about Greg and worrying about Maria's seeing my house. After school I told Donnie I had something else to do again and met Maria at her car. Maria must have sensed that I was still irritated because all the way to our house, she kept saying little things to reassure me. By the time we had pulled up into my driveway, I felt better about us and about the whole Greg business. There was only the laundry and my mother to worry about now.

"Wow, this is a cool place," Maria said, getting out.

I rolled my eyes and opened the front door. Just as I had feared, clothes were strung out all over the living room. I immediately started pulling them down. Maria had a good laugh.

"What are you doing? You're acting like a crazy person."

"I hate the way this all looks."

My mother, who had been preparing dinner, came out of the kitchen, smiling and drying her hands on her apron.

"God, Mom. Do you always have to leave the laundry out like this?"

"Oh, I don't know why you make such a big deal out of it, Sugarbear."

"Hi," she said to Maria and held out her hand. "Aren't you going to introduce me to your friend here?"

"Mom, this is Maria, and stop calling me Sugarbear."

My mother pinched my cheek and shook hands with Maria.

"So nice to meet you. My name's Sage."

"Hello, It's so nice to meet you too, Mrs. Bailey. Your home is cool tucked away in the woods like this."

"Well we like it a lot. Thanks."

My mother seemed to like Maria instantly and I was glad at least to see the two of them hit it off. Both of them being so short and with dark hair, it was sort of a natural. Maria, of course, was younger and more innocent looking. My mother had a mature face but was blessed with a radiant smile.

While they talked in the kitchen, I got rid of the laundry.

"So, what are you kids up to today?" my mother asked when I came back.

"Oh, we're just going to hang out and listen to some music out in the cabin. Maybe we'll go for a walk in the woods and see the big rock."

She smiled at Maria and looked back at me.

"Okay, but why don't you two leave the door open to the cabin, okay, honey? It's a nice sunny day. I'm sure the cabin could stand to be aired out a bit. You don't want to end up smelling like the cabin, that's for sure."

"Cut it out, Mom."

Maria laughed. My mother smiled at me.

"Come on, let's go," I said to Maria.

"Nice meeting you, Mrs. Bailey," she said as we went out the back door. "Your mother's sweet," she said to me as we started toward my father's hunting cabin.

Maria gave me a little peck on my cheek. I was still irritated with my mother and filled with regret at having brought Maria over to my house. I hated being discovered, even if it was true what she had said. Everyone at school smelled of fabric softener and I smelled like campfires.

Nestled back among some pines, we came to the hunting cabin. I opened the door for Maria and followed her in. There were antlers on the walls and several cheesy paintings of deer mounted among the antlers.

"This place is kind of cool, too," she said.

"Yeah, I love the musty smell of stale booze."

"Oh, poor Sugarbear," she said and gave me a kiss on the neck.

I looked back and saw my mom working away through the kitchen storm door. I knew she wasn't one to spy, but she could easily keep an eye on us from that location. There wasn't much room for hanky-panky.

"What do you usually do out here?" Maria asked.

"My father has all his buddies over here during hunting season. They sit around drinking cheap booze and bragging about who shot the biggest buck."

"Do you ever go hunting with them?"

"No, not usually. I have in the past, but I don't see the point of shooting some poor defenseless deer."

"What's your father like?"

"He's all right."

We plopped down on the sofa together.

"He's a corrections officer and he's kind of like that when he comes home. You know, untrusting and distant for the most part. He's always working -- that or playing around with his boat."

I peeled back the curtain and pointed to my father's boat parked next to the cabin.

"Is that him?" Maria said, looking at a picture on the wall.

"Yeah, that's him."

It was a picture of my father with his uniform and cap on.

"He looks like a real tough guy," Maria said.

"Yeah, he's built like a bull, but aside from the corrections officer thing, he's a pretty cool guy. Kind of soft-spoken except when he's mad. He tells me all these stories about what goes on there at the prison."

"Like what?"

"Oh, like when they have to take one of the inmates down to the hole."

"What's the hole?"

"It's solitary confinement. So anyway, I guess they come in with several guards and the first thing they do is tell the guy to get down and spread his arms and legs so they can handcuff him. Well, this one time, my father gives the command and the guy goes nuts. He was a drug addict in there for murder or something and didn't have much to lose. Next thing you know, my father and the other guards are in an all-out battle with this guy. The inmate is kicking and spitting and throwing punches. They finally get the guy down on the ground but he's still going nuts so my father lost his patience and tackled the guy."

"What!?" Maria exclaimed, laughing.

"Yeah, it sounds pretty funny now but I guess it wasn't so funny then. Anyway, they finally got this guy cuffed but afterward he's still screaming about using 'excessive force' and how he'll sue."

"Sounds like it's kind of scary working there," Maria said.

"Well, like I said, my Dad's built like a bull. He's not very tall but you wouldn't want to mess with him."

"Who's this?" Maria asked about another photo.

"That's me with my two older brothers."

"Where are they?"

"They both graduated and moved out a little while back. Jacob is older and is off at college. Noah is stationed in Holland with the Air Force."

Maria put the picture down.

"So now it's just you at home, huh, Sugarbear?"

"Shut up," I said.

Maria laughed and went to peek out the curtains. My mom was washing dishes at the kitchen sink. Maria let the curtain down and kissed me.

"Let's go for a walk in the woods," I said nervously. "I'll show you this cool field and the big rock."

"Okay, the big rock?"

"Yeah, just wait. It's pretty neat."

We made our way a couple hundred yards up the main trail into the forest and eventually ended up in a large open field. The field was several acres and filled with high grass, sumac trees, wild flowers and taller brush. The field sat on a knoll overlooking a beautiful, wooded valley. The mountains were far off in the distance.

A twenty-foot-high boulder sat on the hill among the high grasses and sumac trees and seemed like an island in the middle of that lake of grass.

"Wow, it's amazing!"

"I know. I love it up here. Sometimes I come here just to think or take a nap."

"I can't believe how beautiful this is and that must be the big rock," she said, pointing in its general direction.

"Yeah, you want to go sit on top?"

"We can do that?"

"Yeah, of course. I do it all the time."

From below, I helped her get up and quickly followed. It felt like you could see forever.

"Wow, this is really cool. And scary, too!"

"Don't worry. I've got you."

She smiled and we kissed again.

When we stopped, I placed my arm around her and we gazed out over the forested valley below. While we sat there, I felt completely free and in love.

Time was flying by.

"Now for the fun part," I said.

"What's that?"

"Getting down."

She laughed.

"Oh no. I'm scared."

"Don't worry, I'll go down first and then help you off."

I scampered halfway down and reached up to help. Maria stared down with a nervous look on her face.

"Come on. It's all right."

Tentatively, she inched her way into my arms and we repeated the process one more time.

Back on solid ground, I gave Maria a passionate kiss and we started on our way back to the house hand in hand.

The day had grown late as we walked back down to the house. Inside, I found my mother stoking the wood-burning stove.

"Oh, honey," she said. "Would you go out and bring in some more firewood? I think it's going to be a cold one tonight."

"Can I help?" Maria whispered as we went outside.

"You sure can," I whispered back.

"I think it's really cool that you have a wood-burning stove," Maria said outside. "It does seem like a lot of work to maintain, but very cool."

"Yeah, well, it's not as cool as you think. Only having a wood burner for heat means we have to work our butts off all year long cutting down trees and splitting firewood just so we can stay warm in the cold months."

While I was stacking wood, Maria came over and felt my muscles.

"It seems to have its advantages."

"Yeah, I suppose so, but it's still a bummer. A lot of times in the spring and early fall, after I come home from school, I barely have time to grab a quick bite and then it's out into the woods to work. Weekends, too. It definitely doesn't leave much time to play."

"I still think it's nice," Maria said. "It's sort of a way to bring your family together. I wish we had something like that."

"Yeah that's why we do it, to bring us together," I said sarcastically.

After I dropped off the wood in the living room, Maria insisted on a tour of the house. There wasn't much to it. The downstairs consisted of the kitchen, our living room, a bathroom and my parents' small bedroom.

We went up to my bedroom in the small attic.

"Before my brothers moved out, they slept up here, too."

"Don't you have a TV?" Maria whispered.

"Just the one downstairs. There isn't much time to watch it. And besides, we don't have cable anyway, so there isn't much to watch. Just the three network channels, plus PBS."

"Wow," she said. "You don't even have cable? That's crazy."

"Yeah, well, please don't mention it to anyone at school about that or the wood burner. Most people just have to hit the thermostat when they want to get warm and I don't know anyone else that doesn't have cable."

"Speaking of getting warm," Maria said. "Want to come over to my place again tomorrow?"

"Sure."

She snuggled up to me playfully and we went back downstairs.

When we were at her house the next day, I noticed she had taken down the pictures of Greg. I was wondering if she had destroyed them or simply put them away somewhere, but I was just glad that he wasn't there with us anymore.

"You know what?" Maria asked after we had been there for a spell.

"No, what?"

"My parents asked if you'd like to come over for Thanksgiving dinner on Thursday. Can you?"

"I don't know. I'll have to ask my parents."

Maria rolled over to look at me.

"I hope you can."

"Most of my family is coming by for dinner, so I'll have to let you know later on."

Maria gave me a ride home and I had her drop me off down at the bottom of our driveway.

That night over dinner, I asked my parents about Thanksgiving. Both of them seemed disappointed but ultimately agreed. With my aunts and uncles coming over for the holiday, there wouldn't be an empty house.

On Thanksgiving Day, I walked in to find Maria's father sprawled out on the sofa in the living room. A football game was playing on the TV.

"Justin, you already know my father, Nick, and this is Larry, my sister's boyfriend. Larry, this is Justin."

Larry reached out to shake my hand without standing up.

He was wearing a tie dye t-shirt and looked like he hadn't shaved in a few weeks.

"Good to see you again," Nick said.

"Mr. Gallo, how are you, sir? Thanks for having me over for Thanksgiving dinner."

"Hey, good to have you, son. Please call me Nick. Hey, Maria honey, get him something to drink."

Maria led me into the kitchen. I looked back once. Maria's younger sister and brother were playing video games in the living room and had never bothered to look up.

Out in the kitchen, I said hello to Maria's mother, Ellen, and met her sister, Carmella. They were busy preparing the dinner together. Maria grabbed me a soda and jumped in to help with the meal. I sat there, watching from a chair and talking with them.

"Hey, let's go take a boat ride," Maria said when things were under control.

"Cool," I said, and we started back out through the living room.

"Hey, Justin," Nick said. "Have a seat and help yourself to some calamari."

"It's cool, Dad," Maria said. "We're going to take the boat for a little ride."

"Great idea, I just got it tuned up. I guess it's going to be a little while before your mother has dinner ready anyway."

When we got back to the house about half an hour later, the meal still wasn't ready and Nick and Larry had disappeared into the garage. Maria jumped back in to help with the final preparations. I sat down again and watched from the kitchen table.

When dinner was ready, Maria called to Nick and Larry. They had been looking at Nick's new Harley-Davidson motorcycle. Like Nick, Larry looked a bit like the biker type. They came in a few minutes later, washed their hands, and joined us for dinner.

The dinner was very close to the one my mother always put together and included the turkey, mashed potatoes and gravy, three or four vegetables and pumpkin pie for dessert.

Nick carved the turkey at the table. "So, Justin, do you like dark meat or white meat?" he asked.

"A little of both please, Nick," I replied.

Ellen added, "Maria told us what a wonderful place your family has, complete with wood heat and lots of land. It sounds terrific."

"It may be more romantic when you're not swinging a splitting maul every other day," I countered.

"Well, I loved it and the huge property your parents own," said Maria.

While the women were cleaning up after the meal, I heard the roar of several Harleys arriving outside. Some of Nick's friends had arrived. Nick and Larry went back out to the garage to greet them. A short while later, all of them were in the bar area. There was loud talk and boisterous laughter from that direction. Maria's mom went out to the bar and I heard her speaking with Nick.

"Let's go downstairs to play some pool," Maria said, once the kitchen was cleaned up.

"What's going on up there?" I asked when we were downstairs.

"Oh, my dad and his friends are always up to no good and it gets my mom upset. I don't much care for it either."

While we played pool I heard the party getting into full swing upstairs as someone fired up the jukebox.

"What do you think about drugs?" she asked me while I was racking up the balls.

"I don't know, what have you got?" I asked jokingly. She laughed, but I could see by her expression that she was not happy with the activities upstairs.

"I guess I don't have a problem with it except it always seems to lead to some kind of trouble with my father."

We played a couple games of pool, then settled down to watch a movie. Halfway through the flick, we heard Nick yelling upstairs. Ellen quickly yelled back and soon an argument ensued.

"Oh boy, here we go," Maria said.

There were a couple of loud thumps and it sounded like Nick was getting into it with his biker friends. The struggle spilled out onto the front lawn. We ran upstairs to investigate. Through a small window, I saw Ellen going after Nick. She seemed very upset. Carmella and the kids were trying to throw themselves between their parents. It was a madhouse, with everyone crying and screaming. Some of the neighbors came out on their own lawns.

"What the hell are you looking at?" Nick asked one of them.

"Just waiting for the cops to show up, Nick. As usual."

"Yeah, well, to hell with you all," he said.

A few minutes later, I heard the sound of sirens off in the distance. Nick jumped on his Harley and flew down the road.

Maria and I sat huddled together in the darkened front room and watched from the big picture window as the cops arrived and questioned everyone outside. The red and blue lights from their cars were flashing around on the ceiling and walls. Maria had finally stopped crying. She went for a tissue.

"Wow, this is really crazy. Are you gonna be all right?" I asked when she got back.

"Yeah, I'll be okay. It always ends up this way when my dad gets messed up. He makes a scene and acts like a raving lunatic. The cops come out here to arrest him. He runs off before they arrive. The cops eventually leave and my father comes back with his tail between his legs later on. My mom always forgives him. Then we all pretend like it never happened."

I sat there, not knowing quite what to say. The day had started out so pleasantly. I never expected it to end so dramatically.

Eventually the cops left as did Nick's biker friends. Larry went with them. Maria and I heard Ellen and the kids coming back inside and Maria went to check on them. I decided to follow. Ellen, Carmella and the kids were sitting at the kitchen table playing Monopoly. Ellen's nose was red and swollen.

"You missed all the fun," Carmella said.

Ellen waved Maria over and gave her a hug.

"My sweet little baby. You take good care of her, Justin," she said to me over her daughter's head. She kissed Maria and invited me to sit at the table.

"We're going to go hang in my room, okay, Mom?"

"Sure, hon, sure."

Ellen tried to smile at me.

"Sorry you had to be a part of this, Justin. I can tell you're a real nice boy."

I nodded. Maria and I went to lie on her bed.

Much later, we heard Nick's motorcycle pull back into the driveway. There was the sound of his voice out front. Whatever else had happened while he was away, his return was a lot quieter than his exit.

I checked my watch. It was getting late.

"I'd better get going," I said. "My parents will be expecting me."

Nick was lying on the sofa alone when we went out by the living room. He acknowledged us by holding up his beer but was otherwise silent. We went out to the kitchen.

"Thanks for the great meal," I said to Ellen.

"And the show," Carmella whispered.

Ellen waved me over and gave me a hug.

"Thanks for taking good care of my baby."

"Thank you again," I said.

"I'll walk you outside," Maria said.

"Hey, nice to see you again," Nick said as we went back out through the living room.

"The feeling is mutual, Mr. Gallo," I said.

"You can call me Nick," he said. "And, hey, don't make too much of the action. We have to give the cops some reason to justify their existence."

He winked liked we were buddies.

"You're welcome to come over and spend time with Maria whenever you want, okay?"

"Sure, thanks," I said.

"I think my dad really likes you," Maria said outside.

"I guess that's a good thing," I said.

Maria gave me a big kiss.

"You know what?"

"No, what?"

"My birthday is coming up soon."

"Really? That's great. Happy Birthday. So what are you planning to do?"

"My folks are going to take me out to Prime Grill for dinner. Would you like to come?"

"Sure, if you don't think your parents would mind."

"They don't mind. I already asked them."

"Yeah, sure. That would be cool. I'll just have to work all weekend to get my chores done so I can go."

I got into the car.

"I love you," Maria said, and kissed me.

"I love you, too."

"Hey, call me tomorrow, okay?"

"I will."

She kissed me again before I drove off. I headed home with very mixed feelings. On the one hand, how sweet could life be? Maria had just told me she loved me and her father had said it was cool for me to come over and hang out at their place on the lake any weekend. But there was the drunkenness and the violence, and I hated how it could complicate almost any situation. Of course, being young and in love for the first time, the excitement I felt about being with Maria easily won out.

After doing my chores all weekend, my parents allowed me to use the car on Sunday and I drove over to Maria's place just after dark. With Prime Grill being a high-end steak and sushi joint, everyone was all dressed up. I had on a sports coat and tie.

Maria's parents owned a big luxury passenger van and we went through a bit of chaos getting everyone settled inside comfortably. Ellen sat up front with Nick. The rest of us were in back. Nick had downed two quick cocktails before we left and he immediately turned the stereo up full blast. We hit the road with his singing "Free Bird" at the top of his lungs.

Given the experience of Thanksgiving Day, I viewed his conduct with caution, but so far, so good. The fifteen-minute drive into town went off without a hitch.

As Nick was braking for the first red light in town, I saw a car wheel go flying by us.

"Wow! Did you see that?" Maria asked.

"Yeah, yeah," Nick said.

Then everyone piled over to one side of the van to have a look.

"Boy," Nick said. "That sorry son of a gun is going to be bummed out when he finds out he only has three wheels."

As we were all having a good laugh, gravity took over. The van suddenly listed hard to the rear, driver side corner and a rooster tail of sparks shot up into the sky behind us.

"Damn!" Nick screamed. "That was MY wheel!"

Mirth turned to panic as Nick came to a stop in the middle of the street.

"Come on, everybody. Let's get over on the side of the road."

With cars coming and going around the disabled vehicle, Ellen made sure to get the kids safely off the street first. The rest of us followed. By the time everyone was safe, Nick's comb-over was a disheveled mess. He looked pretty comical.

"Wow!" he said. "That was scary."

"Well, what are we going to do now, Dad," Maria asked. "It's like my birthday dinner is totally ruined."

"No it's not, sweetheart, don't worry about a thing. I've got it handled."

Being up on the latest technology, Nick owned one of those big walkie-talkie-type cell phones and quickly had a limo on the way to pick us up. While we waited, Nick pretended to be driving along again, laughing at the poor sucker who had lost his wheel, then crapping his pants when he realized the tire was actually his. Everyone was in stitches.

By the time the limo arrived, a tow truck had hauled the van off to be repaired. We all hopped into the limo and continued on with the party.

For dinner, a Japanese chef prepared our food right in front of us and flipping bites of food from the grill into our mouths. Nick was exchanging barbs with the chef the entire time.

After the meal, a special birthday presentation with dessert arrived and we all sang "Happy Birthday" to Maria. The people at the tables around us chimed in. Nick had been downing sake all night, but to my surprise the evening ended without a bit of drama.

Maria had her head on my shoulder and a big grin on her face all the way home.

"That was the most perfect evening of my whole life," she whispered to me at one point.

"Me too," I said.

I was so in love with her, and so glad to know that she loved me too. I glanced around the limo. I was even glad about being accepted by her comical and sometimes dysfunctional family.

Five

Later in the winter, wrestling season began, which meant a gang of us packed into a small wrestling room for several hours of practice every day after school. One of the coaches was named Skip Collins. The Skipper, we called him. Tim Johnson was the other coach. The training was top notch, the practices challenging and we became a pretty exceptional team.

There were a bunch of us and every weight class had "wrestle-offs" each week to challenge for the top spot in the weight division. Even though I weighed in at just 105 pounds, I had plenty of competition.

Being buddies on the team, Ted, Ethan and I would always try to wrestle next to each other. There was a lot of kidding around during practice. It was a combination of laid-back joking around and really hard work. We warmed up with stretches, then moved on to a hardcore cardio workout. A lecture followed where we learned new moves and studied the other team's strategies. Then we wrestled. After the wrestling session, we did a warm-down and final stretch before hitting the showers.

I left the first day of practice as I always did, drenched in sweat and tired as hell. My father was a big fan of wrestling and had come by to pick me up. My mom was with him.

"Let's drive out to Hardey's Lake," my father said. "I've got a challenge for you."

"What kind of challenge?" I replied.

My father glanced at me in the rearview mirror.

"If you can beat me around the lake, I'll let you visit Maria for a few hours while we hang out at Gram and Grandpa's."

I had just wrapped up three hours of wrestling practice. The loop around the lake was over eight miles. The last thing I wanted was to run part of a marathon, but for a few hours with Maria, I was ready to do anything.

My father pulled over at one end of the lake near Joe's Pizza. "All right here you go."

I got out and my father started to pull away slowly.

"Hey, aren't you going to get out, too?"

"No, I'm going to have your mom drop me off up ahead. I'm an old man. I need a handicap."

"How far ahead?" I asked, calling after him.

"Oh, about halfway, but don't worry, I'll be walking because I'm an old man."

"Hey, that still isn't fair!" I shouted as he pulled into traffic.

As the car disappeared, I started running as fast as I could. Four miles. That meant I had to double my father's pace in order to beat him. With Maria, the proverbial carrot, in front of me, I raced forward at a blistering pace.

A few miles from Maria's house, I spotted my father. He was huffing and puffing but walking like he didn't have a care in the world. I put on the afterburners and passed him. He acted startled as I flew by.

"Hey, old man," I said with a laugh, looking back.

"Hey," he said, breaking out a smile. "Go ahead and stop at Maria's house. Your mother and I will pick you up in about an hour."

"Don't kill yourself there, Pops."

He smiled and waved his hand at me.

Maria's place was about a mile and a half from the finish line. I jogged up to her front door, drenched in sweat. When Maria answered my knock, I was still doubled over, catching my breath.

"What's going on?" she asked.

I explained about the "race". Maria shook her head as I told her the details. I stood up and gave Maria a kiss.

"Mind if I have a shower?"

"No, of course not. I'll get you a towel."

After I had dried off, the two of us kicked back until my folks arrived.

"Hi, Mr. Bailey," Maria said, when we went out to the driveway to meet them. "You don't look the worse for wear."

My father smiled.

"I let him beat me," he said with a smile.

"Yeah, right, Dad," I said, getting into the car.

Maria waved as we backed out of the driveway.

"See you at school tomorrow," she called out to me.

Several weeks went by when one day, Donnie cornered me before wrestling practice. I hadn't hung out with him or my other friends much since I started going with Maria.

"What's up, dude?" he said. "You don't hang around with your boys anymore?"

"Dude, what can I say? I'm into Maria and she always wants to spend time with me."

"So, ask us over to hang with you."

"I don't think you're getting it. I mean, what are you going to do, hang around and watch us?"

"No way dude. You mean you're actually doing it?"

"No we're playing Scrabble." I said sarcastically.

"Yeah right, I'll bet you are."

Donnie looked like he was ready to make an announcement so I grabbed him and put my hand over his mouth.

"Come on, man. I'm begging you. Keep your mouth zipped about this, all right?"

"Ha, ha," he said. "I get it. Don't blow it for you."

"I mean it, man. Seriously."

"All right, all right. I'm not going to blow it for you. I'm just freakin' jealous, man. I can't believe you're finally getting some action."

"I have to say, we've spent a lot of time together and I love this girl."

"Wow, I can't believe it. Did you say love?" Donnie asked. He slammed his fist into his locker. "I don't believe you."

"Yeah man, I can't stop thinking about her."

"That's just the 'little guy' talking."

"Screw you, dude."

I pushed him. He laughed and pushed me back.

"All right, bro," I said. "I gotta get to wrestling practice. I'll see you later."

"All right, dude, I'll smell you later."

He smiled as he left.

It wasn't long before we had our first wrestling match. It was an away meet and as the team came piling out into the parking lot, the cheerleaders were already on the bus. The coaches sat up by the driver. The cheerleaders sat in the front seats behind them. The wrestlers had the back of the bus. My buddy Ethan took a seat right behind the last row of cheerleaders. As I reached the bus I realized I forgot something.

"Oh, no," I said to one of my teammates. "I forgot my headgear."

By the time I raced back from my locker, the bus was idling and Coach Collins seemed agitated.

"Justin, where the heck have you been?"

"Sorry, coach."

I showed him my headgear.

"I left it in my locker."

"Ten laps," he said, then laughed at the look on my face. "All right, let's get out of here," he said to the driver.

The door closed and the bus lurched forward. The cheerleaders were all chatting away among themselves or listening to music. It was a madhouse in back with the wrestlers.

I noticed Stacy Walcott had taken the seat right in front of mine. Stacy had eyes the color of summer skies and curly blond hair pulled back in a ponytail. She was the prettiest girl in our grade and every guy, including me, was dumbstruck by how drop-dead gorgeous she was. Therefore I was totally shocked when she looked over the seat and smiled at me. I didn't know what to say. We had never communicated before so I just smiled back.

"You got your weight?" Ethan asked me.

"Yeah, dude, but I'm freakin' starving. I haven't eaten a thing all day."

It was a constant fight for me to maintain my weight. Ethan, on the other hand, was a heavyweight and had no upper weight limit. He could eat as much as he wanted.

"You want a piece of this?" he asked and pulled out a delicious-looking cold cut sub.

"You piece of crap," I said, smiling but not happy. "I ought to beat you over the head with that thing."

I heard Stacy giggling in front of us.

"What the heck are you laughing at?" Ethan asked her.

Stacy got on her knees, facing backwards on the seat to talk with us.

"Poor Justin. He hasn't had a meal all day. He looked like he was going to pass out in English class today and you're tempting him with that?"

She pointed at the giant sub.

"Yeah man, you're killing me. I'm lucky to be alive with how hungry I am."

"You want some?" Ethan asked to Stacy.

"Oh man," I said, pretending to die.

Stacy laughed. I watched her, astonished at learning that she had even noticed me during English class. In fact I wouldn't have guessed that she knew I was alive.

The three of us continued talking all the way to our opponent's school.

"Talk with you on the way back," Stacy said, as the cheerleaders started to file off the bus. "Good luck with your match."

"Thanks."

"Good luck with your match," Ethan said in a girl's voice, busting my chops.

"Shut the heck up."

"What, dude? I think Stacy really digs you, man."

"Right. She likes me about as much as I like getting tempted by your sub, you wacko."

Ethan pushed me playfully and we went off to get weighed in. Once that had been done, everyone on the team got to splurge on a pregame meal before our matches began.

That night, I lay awake in bed remembering my conversation with Stacy. Wow. Did the most beautiful girl in our class have a crush on me? It was hard to imagine, but she had seemed completely sincere. This was a real conflict. I had given my heart to Maria and now I had another really hot girl interested in me. I drifted off, thinking of my good fortune but vaguely aware that it could all turn to famine very quickly.

It was not long after that episode that Maria started acting unusually distant. She seemed to avoid me during school and always had errands to run after. One night that week we went out to dinner together. She was being extremely quiet and was nervously picking at her food.

"What's up with you?" I asked.

She looked up from her food.

"I have something I need to tell you."

"Yeah, so what is it."

"So, I've had a crush on Dickie Hellerman ever since we were in junior high school and now he's asked me to go out with him."

I stared at her with a sick feeling in my gut. The girl I thought was my girlfriend was telling me she wanted to be with someone else.

"What do you mean? You told me you loved me."

"I'm sorry Justin," Maria said. "I just didn't know how to tell you. Dickie and I have known each other a long time and I really like him a lot."

Unable to eat another bite of food, I called for the check and drove Maria straight home.

That night I lay awake again, completely torn up. I had been abandoned by the girl I loved and who I thought loved me back. Not only was she dumping me, but she was rejecting me for Dickie Hellerman of all people.

Later on, I stared at the ceiling, unable to think about anything but how the last few months must have been meaningless to Maria.

I called her that night to see if she could explain what had happened to us but her mother said she wasn't at home. At school the next day, Maria continued the avoidance routine with me but that afternoon I finally caught up with her outside of one of her classes.

"Oh, hi," she said, like she was surprised to see me. "Sorry. I haven't been trying to ignore you or anything but you might want to stay away."

"What the heck do you mean by that?"

"I'm sorry, Justin. I mean, I really never meant to hurt you but I am going out with Dickie now and I'm afraid of what he'll do if he sees us together."

"I guess it's true then," I said.

"What's true?"

"What they say about the apple not falling far from the tree. You're picking a guy who's a big, stupid, violent jerk, just like your mother did."

Maria slapped me. Then she looked remorseful. Her eyes welled up with tears.

"I'm sorry," she said. "But you've really got to stay away. You know how he can react. Let's just be friends, okay?"

I ditched my last class, went to the locker room and cried. I had never been in love before Maria. I had never known how much it could hurt. The whole thing just didn't make any sense to me.

That night I went to a basketball game with Donnie and Eli, all torn up over Maria but still convinced I could win her back somehow. We had gone up into the bleachers looking for her, when all of a sudden, Donnie was dragging me back behind the bleachers by the arm.

"Hey!" I said. "What's going on, dude?"

"Sshhh," he said. "There he is!"

"Who?"

"Dickie."

I peered out from the gym corner and saw Dickie going by with Maria. Maria was wearing his black-and-grey varsity football jacket. They were arm in arm. She looked really happy. They both looked really happy. He had a cocky expression on his face.

"Come on," Donnie said. "Let's go somewhere else."

I joined him and Eli as we wandered around in the half darkness, not really knowing what to do. There were cheers from the spectators around me but I was down in the dumps.

"That's so messed up," Eli said, trying to console me. "That is not cool, dumping you like that."

"Please don't get into this, dude," I said.

"Hey, I'm sorry, man," Eli said. "But let's just get out of here and go have some fun. There are all kinds of girls out there, bro."

We went past all the concession stands outside the gym, selling hot dogs and sodas and shirts with the team logo on them. Most everyone we passed was dressed up in the school colors, parents and kids included. A few people had their faces painted black and grey. Victory banners had been planted around the outside. But all I could think about was how much I missed Maria and still wanted to be with her.

Later on Donnie, Eli and I ended up at a party and had been there for about an hour when Donnie came hurrying into the kitchen.

"Damn, they're out in the living room, man."

"Who?"

"Dickie and Maria!"

"Well it was only a matter of time."

"Let's just get out of here," Donnie said.

We went out the back door and snuck around to the front. I stared back at the house as I got into Donnie's car, feeling so bummed out. I went to sleep that night with thoughts going round and round in my head of missing Maria and wanting to see her again. The next morning I woke up feeling awful. I was sick to my stomach from too much cheap beer and sick at heart from being tossed aside.

I dreaded going to my job that night and considered calling in sick. A few weeks earlier I had gotten hired on as a curb runner for a fast food place called the Timber Wagon. They specialized in hamburgers and foot-long hot dogs. My job was to sit out front and take orders from people as their cars pulled into the parking lot. That meant I'd be out there in my silly uniform, worrying about whether someone I knew from school would come in.

I ultimately did the responsible thing and went into work that evening. There were three of us sitting out front, looking dorky in our uniforms, waiting for customers to come in. It was icy cold outside. The chill in the air was almost unbearable.

As dinnertime rolled around, my buddy Troy's Toyota pick-up came down the street and pulled into the parking lot. He was on a date with a girl Mary that I knew. I went out to greet them as they parked.

"Hey guys, this is a surprise. How are you doing tonight?" I asked, trying not to look embarrassed by my uniform.

"Good, we're on our way to the movies and figured we'd stop by for a quick meal before that," Troy said.

"Cool. Hey Mary, don't let this guy make you pay for everything tonight."

She smiled.

"Very funny, Justin," Troy said.

"So what can I order for you two?"

"I'll try a hot dog and a soda," Mary said.

"Same goes for me, Justin," Troy added.

I returned later with their food and we continued to chat.

"So how often do you work here, Justin?" Mary asked.

"Only a few days a week. The money isn't bad and the great part is, I get to wear these awesome uniforms all the time."

They both laughed and I left them alone to eat. I returned later on to clear away their tray and send them off.

"Well, thanks for coming by to visit," I said.

"No problem. Hey, did you hear the story about Dickie Hellerman?" Troy asked.

"No, I didn't. What did he do now?"

Honestly, I wasn't in the mood to hear a story involving Dickie now that he was with Maria, but I listened anyway. I figured it was probably some crazy story and with Dickie, you never knew what to expect.

"Someone told me that he went downtown with a few of his buddies and they were just randomly pulling people out of their cars and beating the crap out of them."

"Wow, that's friggin' crazy!" Mary said.

"I know! I thought the same thing. I mean who would do something like that?" Troy added.

As I stood there listening I had to agree. Who the heck does stuff like that? It's just insane.

"Hey listen, guys, It's getting pretty busy here so I'm gonna have to have to get back to work."

"Oh no problem, dude, thanks for everything. We'll see you later."

"No problem. See you later."

I waved as they left. Inside my mind was going crazy. What was the girl I loved doing with this guy? The more I thought about it, the more it just didn't make sense.

Six

After years of being an introverted kid at school, I had been on kind of a roll there in my junior year, being the class president, in the drama club, belonging to our flawless wrestling team, and of course having Maria as my girl. I had been on top of the world for a few months, but now school was the last place I wanted to be. Oh, I did mingle with my friends and classmates occasionally, and of course participated in my extracurricular activities, but as much as possible, I laid low and kept to myself.

Time went by like this, with me all brokenhearted and mostly avoiding my friends. Then one day, I stopped by the grocery store on the way home and happened to run into Stacy Walcott who was working there as a checker.

Stacy gave me a big smile and acted truly happy to see me when I got in her line.

"How are you, Justin?" she asked as she checked my things.

"Oh, all right," I said.

She kept glancing up at me as she scanned and bagged my things.

"Just all right?"

"Yeah, I'm all right. How are you?"

"I'm not doing too bad. You hardly say hello to me anymore now that wrestling season is over."

"Sorry. I guess I've been a little distracted with school and stuff."

"You do seem kind of down these days."

"Yeah, maybe I am."

Stacy took my cash and gave me my change.

"Hey, I have my break here in a minute. Why don't you stick around and we can catch up before I get back to work."

"Yeah, sure, okay," I said.

"There's a bench out in front. I'll meet you out there in a minute."

I left the store and sat on the bench. Stacy came out soon after.

"It's so good to see you," she said and gave me a playful little shove. "I can't believe you never talk to me at school."

"Sorry. I really have been pretty busy."

"You're still all hung up on Maria, aren't you?"

I looked over at her, then looked away.

"Yeah, I guess."

"You guess?" she retorted, as if the whole world was aware of my misery.

I looked down.

"Go ahead," Stacy said. "You can cry on my shoulder. Tell me what's wrong."

I looked over at her.

"I don't know what to do, Stacy. She said she was so totally in love with me and then runs off with Dickie like it meant nothing. Soon it'll be prom time and I'm just bummed out. I don't even know what to do."

"There's something wrong with that girl, Justin."

"Yeah, you think so?" I said with a touch of sarcasm.

"I know so. We should go to the prom together. You know, that way you can show Maria that you're getting along just fine without her."

I looked out across the parking lot, my brain struggling to digest what I had just heard. Stacy was the "it" girl in my grade. What did she want with me?

"Wait a minute," I said. "Did you just ask me out to the prom, Stacy?"

She blushed and looked down.

"Yes, Justin. Do I have to spell it out for you?"

I was touched. I had never really seen what a sweet and sincere person Stacy could be. She was so gorgeous and self-confident and could have had anybody she wanted. And here she had a secret crush on me. I was shocked.

"Well?" she asked.

"Wow, I think that's an awesome idea, Stacy. I'd love to go with you," I said, perking up.

I chuckled, looking straight ahead.

"What?" she asked.

"Nothing, I just never imagined the prettiest girl in school asking me to the prom."

Stacy swatted playfully at my arm.

"So, do you really want to go?"

"Yeah, sure," I said. "As long you wear the dress and I wear the tux."

She hit my arm again, then gave me a little kiss on the cheek.

"I'd better get back to work."

"Yeah, I'd better get these groceries home to my mom. The ice cream must be completely melted by now."

She giggled and stood up. I stood up with her.

"So I'll see you at school tomorrow," she said and gave me a hug before returning to work.

I drove home with my mind all confused but my head in a cloud. I was elated to have Stacy in my life. If only I wasn't so hung up on Maria.

On prom night, Stacy drove her Volkswagen Jetta to my house. Her car always smelled like pancakes and I'd make fun of her for it but it was way better than driving my parents' car. She came in the house and the two of us posed for pictures after which my mom escorted us outside.

"You two look so nice," she said.

She offered her guidelines on proper conduct for the evening before we took off. Stacy had insisted that I drive so I opened her door for her, then got in and headed down the narrow driveway toward the road. My mother waved as we disappeared.

We drove over to Stacy's from my house and went through the same ritual with her mother. Stacy was wearing a pale pink dress and looked like a super model. I was feeling dashing as I stood next to her in my black tux.

"You guys make such a cute couple," Mrs. Walcott said. I smiled through my secrets, thinking of Maria briefly as Mrs. Walcott was taking pictures.

As we headed off to the prom, our excitement grew. I was swept along by the events of the evening, but I still thought of Maria periodically. I expected to see her with her date in a short while and that almost made me sick to my stomach. It was hard to tell where the dread of seeing Maria left off and the excitement of prom night began.

Our arrival at the festively decorated hotel downtown was met with great fanfare. Camera flashes went off as we entered the hotel. Everywhere I looked there were beautiful girls in dazzling gowns with perfumed hair piled up their heads.

Stacy made sure to have pictures taken of us as we stopped to socialize every few feet along the way. It took us nearly half an hour to reach our seats and the DJ was playing "Every Little Kiss" by Bruce Hornsby as we I sat down. While Stacy mingled with her friends I looked around for any sign of Maria but she did not appear to be present amid all the couples.

Stacy and I sat at a table with a bunch of other couples that we were friends with. After the meal, they held a ceremony to announce the prom queen. Being juniors, we were spectators until it was time to dance.

The first song was a slow one, "That's What Love is All About" by Michael Bolton and Stacy dragged me out on the floor. As we began to dance, I finally spotted Maria dancing nearby with her date. Our eyes met once and we both quickly looked away. Maria had her hair up in a French braid and looked stunning. For me, the two of us being apart still made no sense. I felt like she still loved me. I knew I loved her, but there she was, dancing cheek to cheek with someone else.

I put my arms tighter around Stacy in response. When I saw Maria look my way again, I put my hand at the back of Stacy's neck and kissed her tenderly. As our kiss ended, I gazed intently into Stacy's eyes.

At the end of the night our gang drove over to a prom party at a friend's place. Her father was well off and they had a really nice house close to the high school.

My friends and I had brought our swimsuits and a change of clothes and everyone got ready to party. After making the rounds and talking with people, we went out by the pool and Jacuzzi to hang out. A bunch of people were splashing around in the swimming pool. The back of the house was mostly glass so you could see everyone partying on the inside, too.

With all the fun, I mostly forgot about my feelings for Maria. I was trying my hardest NOT to think of her and Stacy helped as we shared some intimate moments together.

A bit later, as I sat in a lounge chair out by the pool talking with Donnie and Troy. Stacy came up to me.

"Hey, how have you been?"

"Oh, I'm doing great. How about you?"

Stacy sat down next to me.

"Me too. Are you tired?" she asked me.

"A little. Are you?"

"Yeah. I know a room where we can go lie down and fall asleep together."

"I'm all right for now. Let's just party for a little while longer, okay?"

"Sure, okay."

We hung out there together talking with friends as they came and went. The following morning, I awoke with Stacy next to me.

"Wow, I guess I fell asleep."

"Me too," she whispered, still half asleep. "We should get going, huh? The sun is coming up."

"Yeah, let me gather my stuff."

I felt all groggy on the way back home. When Stacy dropped me off, she kissed me and told me what a great time she had and I agreed.

The sun was up by the time I got home and crawled into bed. My father was having some company over that morning. I hoped they wouldn't make a lot of racket down in the living room, but I was so exhausted I never noticed whether they were loud or not.

A few nights later, Maria called me at home.

"Justin, I think I've made a huge mistake."

"What do you mean?" I asked.

"Dickie isn't right for me."

"And you're just realizing this now?" I questioned half angry.

"I'm sorry, honey, I miss you so much."

"Maria, I couldn't understand why we broke up in the first place."

"Can you forgive me?"

I was so angry and confused, but deep inside I still loved her and wanted to be with her.

"Do you think we can get back together?" She asked.

"You know that nothing makes me happier than being with you Maria. I just don't know if I can get over the way you left me for Dickie of all people."

"Justin, I'm so sorry for hurting you. I want you to know that I've been thinking of you constantly since we broke up."

I waited, not knowing what to say to her. She had left me without considering my feelings at all and now that she had realized her big mistake, she wanted me back. I was so angry and confused, but I was still in love with her.

"Do you still love me?" she asked.

"Yeah," I said after a moment's hesitation.

"Yeah?"

"Yes, I still love you, but that's not the point. You really hurt me, Maria."

I felt a little better getting this off of my chest.

"I'm sorry," she repeated.

"You're sorry? Do you have any idea what you've put me through?"

"If you take me back, I'll do whatever I can to make it up to you."

My mind was racing mile a minute.

"Okay, so what do we do now?"

"I'm going to break up with him this weekend. Will you take me back please?"

That would make me the happiest guy in the world, I thought to myself.

"I guess so."

We parted with a plan to go to the movies the next weekend as I had a party at Randy's that night. That was the night Dickie left for Shady Brook after crashing Randy's party.

Seven

Now that Dickie was away at rehab, and even though Maria had not had the chance to talk to him to break off their relationship, Maria and I kept our promise to each other and started seeing each other right away. We hung out most days after school with frequent visits to her house. We even went to a movie.

One afternoon as I was leaving school with Maria, we came across Stacy in the parking lot. She smiled weakly from several cars over and quickly turned the other way. I felt like hell. The shoe was on the other foot all of a sudden. Stacy was hurt and I was being the jerk.

That night I called to talk with Stacy.

"I'm sorry," I told her straight off.

"I guess I knew it was coming," she said.

"Stacy, it's all my fault and I'm sorry."

I heard nothing but silence.

"Listen, Justin, I've got to go."

"Okay, I'm sorry. Goodbye."

I lay there in the dark, not liking myself very much.

It was not long after my phone call with Stacy that word got around school that Dickie would be home from Shady Brook at the end of the week. Now I was beginning to get a little nervous.

Dickie was returning home, expecting that Maria and he would continue where they had left off before he was taken away.

When I spoke to Maria, she said, "I'll need some time to break it off after Dickie gets back. I'm sorry to have to put you through all of this. I love you, Justin."

"I love you, too."

My mind was racing. On one hand I was finally back with the love of my life, but on the other hand, the sadness I felt having been abandoned still weighed heavy on my mind.

That following afternoon as I arrived home from school, the phone rang. My mother answered it, then cupped the phone.

"It's some guy named Dickie Hellerman."

Terrified, I took the phone and went outside.

"Yeah," I said.

"Is this Justin?"

"Yeah, who's this?"

"It's Dickie, I heard you were going out with my girlfriend while I was away."

"Who said that?"

"Don't screw with me, Justin."

I paced in silence.

"It's cool," he said. "I'll be back at school on Monday and I want to sit down with you so we can clear this up, okay? I don't want any more trouble."

"Yeah, sure, okay," I said.

"And don't be trying to see her anymore, okay?"

"Yeah, sure," I said again.

I got off and went in to hang up the phone.

"What was that about?" my mother asked.

"Nothing."

"Nothing?" my mother asked.

"Yeah, nothing. Just some guy at school wanting to know something."

All Sunday, I couldn't stop thinking about meeting Dickie at school on Monday. He wanted to have a talk. I wanted to be on another planet.

I thought back to another incident involving Dickie. One day while some of us were hanging around in the gymnasium between classes, Dickie and Troy were messing around. Dickie was calling Troy lewd names and saying things about his mom's heritage (Troy's mom was Latino). Dickie was calling him a "spic." Troy didn't respond very well and a scuffle started. I stood there watching this with my other friends, plus some guys from the football team. One of Dickie's friends admitted that it wasn't a good idea to get into it with Dickie, because once you got him started, he was a raving lunatic and wouldn't stop.

Regarding the fight, a couple of guys ended up prying them apart, but I never forgot the statement about not getting into it with Dickie. Troy was no one to mess with either, and Dickie taunted him for no reason. He was willing to fight over just about anything.

On Monday, I was getting some books out of my locker when Dickie suddenly appeared at my shoulder.

"Hey, Justin."

He pretended to straighten my collar.

"You haven't been avoiding me, have you?"

He was smiling, but there was nothing humorous about his attitude. I closed my locker and started to leave.

"Whoa, buddy," he said and grabbed my arm. "I said we're going to have a little chat, remember?"

"I have to get to my class before the bell rings."

"I get it. So I'll just plan to see you out behind the gym during lunch break. If you don't show up, I'll come looking for you."

I started to leave again.

"And right after the bell rings," he called after me. "I don't want to be waiting around for you, dude."

Over the next two hours, I walked around school, keeping all the fear and anxiety bottled up inside of me. There were thoughts of running away or going to the cops or even to the principal, but I dismissed all these ideas in the end. They would only make things worse and would only delay the inevitable. I had seen what Dickie was like when he got angry.

Dickie was waiting for me when I went around to the back of the gym. He smiled his not-so-pleasant smile.

"So you were hanging out with my girlfriend while I was away."

I nodded. My heart was racing.

"So what did you do with her?"

"Nothing, man."

"Nothing, huh? That's not what I heard. One of my friends told me he saw you making out with her at the movies."

I stared with no answer.

"Is that true?"

"We went to the movies once. That was it."

"Yeah, that was it, huh?"

"Yeah, that was it. I swear."

"Well don't you ever so much as look at her again. You got it? You see us coming, you look the other way. I'm not kidding."

For the rest of that day, I pretended everything was cool each time I ran into one of my friends. Secretly I was pretty shaken up. When Donnie took me home from school that afternoon, he kept bugging me to tell him about the confrontation.

"It was no big deal," I said.

I didn't want to talk about it. I didn't want him talking about it. I didn't need my problems spread all around school.

The next day, I was talking with some friends before my afternoon history class when Maria came up to me. As we began to talk, Dickie walked up to confront me.

"So that's it, huh?" Dickie screamed, "Maria says you're the one she wants to be with. Well that's just great, you deserve each other."

Hearing Dickie yelling, my gym teacher came out of the crowd.

"What's going on here?" he asked.

He looked from us to Dickie and back at us again.

"I said, what's going on here, Justin?"

"Nothing."

"Dickie?"

"Yeah, nothing, coach. I was just having a little chat with these two lovebirds."

"Okay everyone, just move on, you hear me?"

Dickie started down the hallway but looked over his shoulder, shaking his head and smiled one of his menacing smiles at me.

Eight

The next week, I noticed Dickie walking around school with a new girl. I also noticed Stacy was getting chummy with one of my old buddies. I was relieved at seeing both of these things. I really hadn't liked myself much for the way I treated Stacy and with a new girl, it seemed like Dickie was happy. My life settled down for a few days and I took time to reflect on the more positive times that year.

I had come to love being in the drama club more than anything else. For me, acting class was like going on summer vacation every afternoon. It was like getting paid to goof off and have fun. Our teacher, Mrs. Collins, was the wife of my wrestling coach, the Skipper, and she really appreciated the work I did. In Mrs. Collins's eyes, I could do no wrong, so I always left that class feeling as good as I could possibly feel about myself and the world.

Another day, as we neared the end of the semester, I noticed the yearbook staff making the rounds for the senior yearbook. Thinking it would be funny to be in as many pictures as possible, whenever I saw the camera crew going by outside of class, I made up an excuse about needing to use the bathroom or something and chased after them. One of their tasks was to take photos of all the students in their homeroom classes and I got my face into nearly every one of those shots for my grade.

I smiled every time I thought of us signing our yearbooks the following year. As class president and a member of both the drama club and wrestling team, I was sure to have my face in a bunch of photos, but with my being in everyone's homeroom picture, I was going be the laugh of the class.

That afternoon, I arrived home from school to find my mother gone on an errand. The house was empty. She had left me a note with a number of chores that needed to be done.

I changed clothes and was halfway out the door when the phone rang. I ran into the house and answered it, hoping it was Maria. Instead, I heard someone breathing on the other end of the line. Then it went dead.

My mother came home a little before five. I was up in my room doing some homework. She poked her head up the stairs.

"Hi, Sugarbear," she said. "How is everything with you?"

I looked over at her.

"I'm fine, Mom."

"Okay. Well, I'll be downstairs, cooking dinner."

A short while later, I heard the phone ring again. My mother answered it. I heard her say "hello" several times and then hang up. There was a long pause before she went back to chopping away at her cutting board.

At lunch the next day, I noticed Dickie smiling at me from the far side of the cafeteria and lost my appetite. Mostly I fiddled around with my food. I looked up a few times and found Dickie still staring at me. He was talking to a couple of his friends but staring and smiling at me the whole time.

I went to school the next day just basically wanting to get through the day without incident. As I arrived in my English class, I discovered that would not be the case. The teacher, Mr. Lucas, said hello to us all and went into a spiel about the impending Moving Up Day ceremony.

"It's a day you will all remember," he concluded. "A day when your junior class president stands before the entire school and gives a speech, acknowledging the outstanding achievements of the departing senior class, bidding farewell to all of them and offering inspiration to all the juniors who will be moving up to take their place in the coming year. I assume you've been preparing your speech for this momentous occasion, Mr. Bailey."

The whole class looked over at me.

"Um, I'm supposed to give a speech?" I replied, half in a daze.

"Um, yeah," Mr. Lucas said, poking fun at me as everyone laughed.

"I thought being class president was so I could get my picture in the yearbook a bunch of times."

There was more laughter and snickering.

"Honestly, I didn't know I had to give a speech, especially not in front of the whole school. Maybe as president I can make somebody else do it."

The laughter continued.

When the bell rang at the end of the hour, I lagged behind while everyone else filed out. Mr. Lucas was organizing his desk as I went up to him. He was an imposing figure to me; tall and thin and very stern-looking. What was left of his balding hair had turned salt and pepper and he always seemed to speak in perfect English.

"So, Mr. Bailey, shall I assume that, up until now, you have not been preparing a speech."

"No, no sir, I have not."

He looked up from his organizing.

"Well, it's really nothing to worry about. You'll only be giving this speech in front of the entire student body, faculty and administrative staff dressed in your finest suit, that's all."

I felt sick at the thought.

"Well, speak up, Justin. What's on your mind?"

"Well, I was wondering if you could give me a hand, you know, with writing the speech."

"I guess, you know, I could."

He stared at me for a moment.

"I'll tell what. Why don't I write a pass for your study hall tomorrow and we'll see what we can work up together."

"Really, are you kidding me?"

"Really," he said. "I'm not *kidding* you and we really need to make sure the word "really" isn't in the speech anywhere."

He smiled.

"So, we'll see you here tomorrow afternoon, Mr. Bailey."

"Thanks," I said, and left feeling at least somewhat comforted. I had no doubt Mr. Lucas could help me write a great speech. Then all I had to do was get up and face the entire student body.

The following afternoon, Mr. Lucas helped me identify some compelling themes for the speech, mostly about the renewal of life and how one generation replaced another. Then he left me to work on it alone. When he returned half an hour later, he critiqued what I had written and encouraged me to polish it up at home that evening.

The next day, I took my speech in to my English class and placed it on Mr. Lucas's desk at the end of class. He read though it quickly and made a few notes.

"You're getting there, Justin. Why don't you polish it one more time and we'll have a look again tomorrow."

He smiled as though he were witnessing my rite of passage.

The next day at the end of class, he quickly breezed through my speech again.

"This will do just fine," he said. "Now all you need to do is get up in front of the entire world and sound like a Roman orator."

"Oh man," I said. "I was feeling all right until you put it like that. What have I gotten myself into?"

Mr. Lucas laughed.

"These life experiences are all a matter of building character, young man."

I went home feeling sick about life's experiences and building character.-

The next morning, I put on a sports coat and tie and went to school. All that day, I was stressed out over the impending ceremony. A little while before it was time for my speech, I went backstage in the auditorium and paced back and forth behind the curtain. On the other side, the seats were filling up. I peeked out several times. The senior class filled the front rows. Mr. Lucas saw me and smiled. Maria waved and winked at me.

When it was time for my speech, I walked out to the microphone terrified. A silence fell over the crowd. I attempted to speak and realized with a panic that I had cottonmouth. I wished that I could reach for a glass of water and take a big gulp. Out in the crowd, I noticed Mr. Lucas. He gave me a thumbs-up, as if to say, "you can do it, son." I looked down at my speech and started to speak.

"Ladies and gentlemen, thank you very much for being here today on this memorable occasion."

The words Mr. Lucas had helped me to hone flowed off my tongue as if I were a professional speaker.

"Life is always moving forward, one generation replacing another. As the seniors move on into the world, they take our hopes with them. As they look back, we are here as a vessel for their fondest memories. We will always be fellow alumni of this great school."

I concluded my speech by thanking the senior class for being our friends and helping us to grow and learn.

"And we, the Class of 1990, and the entire school would like to thank you and bid you a fond farewell."

At the conclusion of my speech, the auditorium broke out in applause and I felt like the man. At the conclusion of the ceremony, I went down into the audience feeling very relieved and many came to congratulate me.

"Way to go, Justin," Bill Simpson said. "You know, I'm almost going to miss you."

He looked at his friends and said jokingly, "Almost."

"Ha Ha, very funny, Bill."

As they went off, other members of the student body came up to greet and congratulate me and Maria came over and gave me a big hug. I never even noticed if Dickie made it to the event.

In fact, in the week that followed, I saw little of Dickie and assumed he was all caught up with the upcoming graduation ceremonies. Soon enough he'd be gone and I could finally forget about him. There was word of his getting back together with his girl or something like that. Whatever the reason, I was happy to avoid any confrontation.

Nine

On graduation day, my friends and I mostly hung around the fringes of the rituals and watched. Given the nice weather, the ceremony took place on the football field. The stands were filled with family and loved ones. I watched with great excitement as Maria crossed the platform and received her diploma. Nick and Ellen were snapping photos of her, Ellen crying and Nick being the proud father.

Then the moment was gone and the stadium slowly emptied out. A feeling of nostalgia hung in the air. I had many friends in the senior class and was kind of sad to see them go. I also felt excited. School was now over until fall. Summertime had started and my mind was filled with expectations for the fun that Maria and I and our friends were about to share.

My parents were away visiting family in upstate New York and had left me their car. It had been prearranged for me to stay at Maria's place and the two of us went back there to get ready for that day's events.

We drove around and visited quite a few friends that afternoon and eventually decided to stop off at Bill Simpson's party with some others. He was having a big party out at the Hardey's Lake Firehouse. There was only one problem -- Dickie was there tending bar. Maria and I walked around for a bit, trying to have a good time but Dickie was staring us down the entire time. Feeling very uncomfortable, we left.

Our next stop was at Lindsay Butler's party near Lake Welton. It was a happening scene. My friend Donnie lived next door and the two parties had basically merged into one.

Donnie was with a bunch of our friends and pouring a beer for himself in a huge tent straddling the two properties.

"Hey, are we gonna have a blast tonight or what, bro?" Donnie asked as we approached.

He handed Maria and me each a beer. As Donnie served someone else a beer, I glanced at Maria. She winked at me. Donnie was looking a bit drunk and she had noticed it, too.

"So, what do you think, bro?" Donnie said, coming back to our conversation.

"Yeah, it's going to be cool."

I toasted to him, and Maria and I headed back outside with our beers. Donnie came out a short time later and asked if we wanted to check out his place next door.

As we were walking along he said, "I'm kind of buzzed up, dude."

"Yeah, you look kind of buzzed up, too."

Donnie kind of stumbled and Maria and I laughed.

"Hey, I need a pack of smokes. Can you drive me down to the store so I can get some?"

"Are you okay with that?" I asked Maria.

"Sure."

"You don't want to come?"

"No, I'll stay here and hang with my friends. I'll see you when you get back. Please drive safely."

Maria gave me a kiss and disappeared into the crowd.

Donnie and I drove along talking about all of the other cool parties that were happening that weekend. We spoke of the parties that we had already been to as well.

"Hey," he said when he got back into the car. "Let's go check out the party at Tracy Chambers's place. I hear it's really a cool one."

Feeling a bit anxious about leaving Maria behind, I went along reluctantly and ended up staying for half an hour. I finally had to drag Donnie out to the car and we drove back to Lindsay's party.

"Where have you been?" Maria asked, as soon as we appeared.

I explained.

"God, you were gone for a long time, honey."

"I'm sorry, babe."

She kissed me.

"I thought we were supposed to be celebrating together."

I could see that she wasn't happy by my being gone so long.

"Okay, I'm sorry," I said. "I'm gonna blame it on Donnie, though."

She slugged my arm playfully and gave me a kiss. A bottle of whiskey came around and we both had a swig with a chaser of Coke. I could feel the tingle in my jaw as I forced it down.

"God, that stuff is awful," I said as I coughed.

"Yeah, I won't be drinking any more of that."

"Me, neither."

I made it a point to stay as level-headed as possible. I had been drunk in the past and really didn't enjoy the hangover. Plus I was responsible for getting Maria and me home safely.

Later on Donnie stumbled up and told me that Kenny Lombardi was sick and needed a ride home.

"Can you do it, bro?"

"Yeah," I said, and went to find Maria.

She wasn't very happy with the news.

"Look, I'll be right back. We're only driving over to Oak Trail."

"You were gone almost an hour last time."

"No I wasn't. Anyway, you're welcome to come along if you want."

"No, I'm just going to stay here with my friends. I'm having a lot of fun."

"Are you sure?"

"Totally."

She went off into the crowd of people and I hit the road with Donnie, Kenny and a couple of other people. Everyone was drinking around me. Donnie had brought along a bottle of cheap beer and they were passing it around the car.

"Just be cool, all right, you guys?" I asked. "I don't want to get pulled over for an open container and end up in jail tonight."

They were all laughing and thinking it was funny, everyone except for Kenny. He looked ready to vomit on my back seat. I don't think he was much of a drinker.

After dropping him at home, we headed back to Lindsay's party. When we got back, the sun was setting and I parked out on the street. Donnie reached over and grabbed my arm.

"Hey, bro, if my parents come home and see me smashed, they're going to kill me. Do you think I can use your dad's cabin for a place to crash tonight?"

"Are you out of your mind dude? My parents will kill me."

"Your parents are out of town, aren't they?"

"Yeah, but they could come back any minute and if they see people in the cabin, they'll ground me forever. Anyway I promised not to be there while they are away."

"Hey, I'll be cool."

I looked over at him.

"All right. I'll stop by and open the cabin right now, but if you come over, there's no partying and you've got to be out as early as possible."

When the car was empty I drove over to my house, somewhat relieved to see my parents were still gone. I parked the car over by the cabin, turned on the lights inside, and hurried back to Lindsay's place.

When I arrived I was told that a lot of people at the party had gone down to Lake Welton on foot, Maria included. I ran to catch up with her and came across a bunch of other people on their way back.

"Have you seen Maria lately?" I asked them.

"I think she left," a girl said.

She looked at the others. They all sort of shrugged.

"Yeah, I didn't see her down there," someone said.

I started walking back. I came across Donnie and some other friends.

"Hey guys, have any of you seen Maria lately?"

"No," Donnie said. "But listen. A few guys left and decided to head over to your place."

"Oh, no," I said. "This isn't the YMCA. I don't want to be housing a bunch of people tonight."

"It's just a couple of people, man."

"Damn it," I said, and ran back to my car.

After a frantic drive home in the dark, I was relieved to find no one there. It must have been a hoax. I drove back to find Maria. I knew she had to be upset. As I drove along, I found her walking alongside the road, about a half a mile down from Lindsay's place. Maria ignored me when I pulled up beside her. I jumped out of the car, but she pulled away when I grabbed her arm.

"Hey, what are you doing? It's dark out here. You could get hit by a car or something."

"You don't even want to be with me!" she screamed.

"What are you talking about?"

"Don't play dumb, Justin. You have hardly spent a single minute with me this whole night."

"Babe, I've been looking all over for you!"

"You haven't paid attention to me all night."

Maria started crying.

"Hey, come on. I've only been thinking of you. It's not my fault I've got a bunch of crazy people for friends. C'mon, honey, I love you."

"Yeah?"

"Of course. I've just been dealing with all these knucklehead drunk people. I heard they were going over to my dad's cabin and it sort of freaked me out."

"What?"

"Yeah, I'm serious."

"So you're not mad at me?"

"No, why would I be mad at you? Besides it's a beautiful night. Look all the stars are out."

I grabbed her and kissed her passionately.

"Hey, come on," I said. "Let's go by my house and grab a sleeping bag or two. Then we'll come back to the party and hang out, okay?"

"Okay," she said. "I'd like to spend the night there, if it's all right with you."

"No problem, babe."

We went to my place, grabbed a couple of pillows and sleeping bags and headed back to Lindsay's party. There were cars all over the place by this point, so we parked way down the street and started back to the party on foot. We were soon approached by Mark and Bill. It was obvious they were uptight.

"Hey, dude," Mark said. "You'd better steer clear of Dickie. He's been talking about beating the crap out of you since he got to the party."

"Yeah, it might be a good idea to lay low," Bill said. "But don't worry. We'll jump in if he gets out of control."

"This must be my lucky day," I said nervously, as my heart pounded.

"Hey sometimes it's a skill to be lucky," Mark said sarcastically.

All of a sudden I heard rapid footsteps from behind us and turned around to find Dickie taking a sucker punch at me. I ducked. Maria screamed. My friend Troy was fast on Dickie's heels and grabbed him. Mark and Bill gave Troy a hand. Dickie was drunk and struggling to get free.

"Just leave him alone," Troy said.

Then suddenly Dickie was all laughs.

"Oh, big tough guy now."

"Big enough to deal with you," Troy told him in a stern tone. "So if you want some trouble, just go pick on somebody your own size."

Dickie laughed and went off with a bottle of whiskey in one hand. Troy, Mark and Bill walked us back to the party.

"Are you going to be all right?" Troy asked.

"Yeah, I guess. It's not going to be much fun playing keep-away-from-Dickie, though."

"Maybe we should just leave," Maria said.

"No, he won't mess with you guys anymore," Bill said. "Just come find us if he gives you any more trouble."

The party was really happening now, but everywhere I went, Dickie followed. If we left Lindsay's place and went next door to Donnie's, Dickie was in the background, staring. I spent the next couple of hours moving from one place to another and looking over my shoulder.

At one point, Maria went off with a couple of her friends and I headed over to Donnie's place. Dickie saw his chance and came toward me with fists clenched. I tried to disappear into the crowd but he caught up with me.

"Hey, hey," he said and pulled me around by my arm. "You know what? I'm just about this close to kicking your ass."

He held up his hand, with his thumb and index finger barely apart.

"Oh, but that's right. I can't. I'm not supposed to deck you because you're so little. You need your friends to stick up for you. Boy, I'd like to cock back and nail you right now."

He pretended to take a swing at me. I turned and walked away as fast as I could to find Maria. She was sitting with some of her friends in the tent. As I was telling her about Dickie, he came in with his bottle of whiskey. From a safe distance, I watched him offer a sip to Bill. Bill took a sip and winced.

"Dude, that's awful. I can never get used to the taste," Bill said.

He passed it back to Dickie.

"No problem for me, man. I don't even need a chaser."

Dickie took another slug like it was a badge of honor and wiped his chin off with his arm.

"You'd better be careful with that stuff Dickie," Bill said.

"Don't worry about it," Dickie bragged. "It's no problem."

I saw Dickie getting lost in conversation with Mark and Bill and whispered to Maria.

"Let's get out of here while we can and take a walk."

I figured we had slipped out of the tent unseen but as we started down the hill toward the highway, I heard Dickie and one of his friends, Gary, coming up behind us. Gary was banging a big stick on the asphalt or something.

"Pussy!" I heard Dickie scream from a distance.

"Don't look back," I said to Maria.

As we hurried forward, one of them launched an empty bottle of beer that flew by our heads. It broke a few feet ahead of us. Maria wasn't wearing any shoes at the time so I helped her get around all the glass. I was in a panic and unsure of what to do next. Dickie and his buddy were almost on top of us.

Just then, Troy came running down the hill.

"What's wrong with you, Dickie?" Troy yelled. "I told you to leave him alone."

"Hey, we're cool, man," Dickie said with a look at me.

"We're just out for a little walk, right, pussy?"

Dickie came up and used his foot to trip me. Troy shoved Dickie.

"I told you to leave him alone."

"Come on, let's go back to the party," Troy said to us.

We followed the road the long way back to the party. I felt somewhat safe with Troy there but the adrenalin was still pumping in my brain and Dickie and Gary were still on our heels.

"Hey," Dickie said. "Your girlfriend's a real friggin' slut. First she's banging Greg, then you and me both. I wonder who's next."

Maria became hysterical at hearing Dickie's vulgar comments. That got Dickie and Gary laughing. I started to turn back, but Troy grabbed me.

"Just keep going," he said.

I put my arm around Maria and looked back at Dickie, feeling a combination of fear and frustration.

"Yeah, she sure has a nice little rack on her. It's too bad she bangs everyone she knows."

At that point I lost my patience and turned to face him. I was sick and tired of him bullying me around and hearing his demented comments.

"You know what, you're nothing but a no-good drunken bum and if you would just quit getting drunk all the time, you'd actually be a decent person."

Dickie started after me at that point, but Troy stopped him.

"Who the hell do you think you're talkin' to like that?" Dickie screamed.

The spray from his spit had hit me in the face from five feet away.

Totally losing it now, Dickie came charging at me like a raging bull. Troy got between us. Even Gary was trying to restrain Dickie now.

"I'll kill you, I ain't no drunken bum!"

"All right, all right, just drop it," Troy said.

"I'll freakin' kill him! I'll freakin' kill you, you punk!"

The veins were popping out of his forehead. He was wrestling to get free of Troy and Gary like a wild animal.

"Justin, just get the hell out of here," Troy screamed. "I'll try to hold as long as I can but he's gonna kill you if he gets loose!"

Maria and I hauled ass back to the party with the sounds of Dickie screaming and hollering behind us. "I'm gonna kill you...I ain't no drunken bum!"

Maria headed inside the tent to be with her friends. In shock from Dickie's display of hatred, and fearful of what he would do if he found me again, I raced on to my car and took off. I was in such a hurry that I nailed a road sign as I backed out of the space.

Relieved to be away from Dickie's raving lunacy, I headed home to the safety of my own house. There was a feeling of concern about Maria but what could I do with Dickie coming after me?

What a friggin' nightmare! I thought I had seen the worst of his rage and evil, but that look in his eyes tonight was on another level. I had never seen anyone so crazy in all of my life. Now I had experienced what the cops must have when dealing with Dickie at Randy's party.

Once home, I went out to check on the cabin. No one had come to spend the night. Relieved by that, I turned out the lights and locked the door.

Back at the house, I checked the clock. It was already well past four in the morning. My father had left me a bunch of chores to do so I decided to take a shower and get them done before they arrived back later that day. Then maybe I could get some sleep. I spent a good twenty minutes in the shower, washing off the lousy feelings and trying to regain my composure.

Ten

Finally out of the shower and drying my hair, I heard a car down at the end of our long driveway. My mind flashed through the range of possibilities. It might be my folks arriving home from their trip. It might be someone from the party coming to crash in the cabin. I was hoping it was Maria. After leaving the party so abruptly, it would be nice to see her.

As I hurriedly threw on some shorts, a sweatshirt and a pair of sneakers, I noticed the dead silence outside. I had expected a car pulling up in the driveway, but all was quiet. Curious more than concerned, I walked from the front of the house to where I could see the driveway. Dawn had set in and the landscape was growing lighter by the minute.

Plain as day, I noticed Dickie at the bottom of the driveway. He was down there, taking a leak.

"Dickie, I'm not gonna fight you, man," I called out, trying to reason with him. "Let's just settle this peacefully."

Dickie finished and started up the driveway toward me, cracking his knuckles. Apparently, my words had fallen on deaf ears.

"I ain't no drunken bum," he said. "Do you hear that, Justin? And you're gonna apologize."

"Dickie, I'm sorry, man."

99

Filled with fear, I ran into the house and grabbed my father's .22 pistol. I couldn't believe he was here. I was all alone with nobody to stop him from hurting me. After all the horrible events I'd seen of Dickie fighting other people, and now he was here at MY home. When I came back outside, Dickie was halfway up the gravel driveway. I pulled the pistol out of its holster and held it in the air to try and scare him off. Dickie continued up the driveway with his fists clenched in rage.

"I ain't no drunken bum. You got that?"

Thoughts raced through my head of Dickie's trying to kick out the window of the police car at Randy's party. Petrified and confused in equal measures, I ran over to the patio and hid the pistol under a folding chair. When I turned back, Dickie was nearly upon me. I held up my hands and tried to be submissive.

"I'm sorry, Dickie. You're no drunken bum. Look, let's just settle this thing peacefully, okay?"

He kept coming nearer. I started to back up.

"We're going to settle things, all right," he said, and grabbed me by the neck of my sweatshirt. I felt myself lifted off the ground momentarily. Dickie started relentlessly beating me on my face and head.

"I ain't no drunken bum, all right? I ain't no drunken bum."

"I'm sorry," I repeated, as I endured his constant torture. "I'm sorry. I didn't mean to piss you off, man."

"Yeah? Well, you did."

He shook me like a rag doll and beat on me more and more. His fists came at me from every direction and his fury was unending. The more I apologized the more he punched me in the face.

Somehow I broke free and backed my way toward the house. Dickie followed me step for step. My back hit hard against the front door, stopping my retreat. The look on Dickie's face was that of a madman. His jaw muscles were working away and he was breathing heavily with rage.

Dickie banged the back of my head into the door with a force that was so great, the door flew open and both of us went tumbling into the living room. Somehow we ended up on the couch with Dickie on top of me. The punches kept coming, anywhere he could land them. He must have been chewing tobacco or something because I felt and tasted it as it hit my lip. I turned and spat it out. My nose and mouth had begun to swell. I felt blood trickling down my throat. The punches came at me in a never-ending flurry of flying fists.

Somehow I managed to kick him off, but he quickly had me up against a nearby wall, one hand on my sweatshirt, the other one hitting me repeatedly in the face.

Then, as if he had experienced a revelation, Dickie suddenly stopped.

Confused and near a concussion, I grabbed his arm.

"Why don't we talk this over," I said, insanely expecting diplomacy to work at this juncture with this monster. My mind was all over the place with fear and panic.

Dickie pulled his arm free.

"Naw, I just want to go outside and shoot a couple rounds."

Again hopeful that his anger had been spent, and willing to do anything to appease him, I followed Dickie outside. On my way past the folding chair, I grabbed the gun. Dickie was headed in the general direction of my father's makeshift target range. I followed with this ogre stumbling along in front of me and removed the gun from its holster.

Then all of a sudden, for reasons I'll never understand, Dickie turned and came at me again.

"You know what? You're too much of a pussy to shoot me."

This didn't make any sense to me. In fear, I started backing up again. Dickie followed me again. I was struggling to free the safety when Dickie shoved me.

"Go on," he said with menace. "You know it would be self-defense."

As he came at me with his fist cocked, I finally got the safety off, clenched hold of the pistol and fired a shot in the air. Dickie looked startled at first by the sound, but then he seemed more enraged.

He came at me filled with anger, and he quickly had my back up against the front of the house. As Dickie was reaching out to hit me in the face, I reflexively fired a shot in his general direction. I thought it must have hit him in the gut but he kept coming at me like nothing had happened. When he clenched his fist and began to throw a punch, I shot again and this time his head jerked back violently. Blood spurted out of his face. He fell to the ground, lifeless. I saw blood pouring out onto the concrete patio.

I ran into the house in a panic and dialed 911. A woman answered the call and I told her what had happened. She kept telling me to slow down. I was in shock and hardly able to recognize my own voice.

Then a policeman came on the line. He asked me for my phone number and location. I gave him the information and said that I'd meet him down at the base of the driveway.

I walked the hundred yards down our gravel driveway to the bottom of the hill. Trees hung over the driveway and camouflaged the morning sun. I was in a daze. Just as I reached Quarry Road, a car came by. It was Bill Simpson in his old beat-up Monte Carlo. He braked to a halt and jumped out.

"What the hell is going on? Where's Dickie?"

"I shot him. I think he's dead."

Bill fell down to his knees and started crying.

"How did Dickie get to my house, Bill?"

"Oh my God!" Bill screamed "I brought him to your place. You don't understand. When you left the party, Dickie was going around like a mental patient asking every guy he knew to give him a ride to your house. I just dropped him off so he could screw with you a bit. I didn't think he'd do that to your head. Dude, you look really messed up. Damn it, you didn't have to shoot him. Oh, my God! Dickie's dead! I can't believe it!"

After he had cried for a spell, Bill came to his senses and stood up. He wiped at his tears with his hands before he climbed back into his Monte Carlo. Once he had his car pulled around the other way, he stopped in front of me.

"I was never here!" he said, with a finger pointed in my direction. I watched him peel out and race down the road out of sight.

About fifteen minutes later, a parade of cop cars and ambulances came slowly up the road, with all their lights going but their sirens off, I assumed out of respect for the hour. There were a handful of local cops, some state troopers, and several ambulances. The whole parade stopped and the cops got out. One of the local guys came up and quickly searched me for weapons.

"I'm Officer Miller," he said. "Where's the body?"

"Up there. At my house," I said, and pointed up the driveway.

He helped me into the back of his squad car and we headed up toward the house. The caravan of cruisers and ambulances came up the hill after us. I was left in back while the cops had a look at Dickie. Then Officer Miller came over and read me my Miranda rights. I was handcuffed and placed back in his cruiser. He pulled his cruiser over next to the cabin and went back to Dickie's body. About thirty minutes later, Miller came over with a plainclothes officer and opened the door. The plainclothes officer had gray hair, parted to one side. His suit was dated. He acted very cordial.

"I'm Trooper Albert," he said. "Do you have any ID?"

"It's in the house."

I explained where and someone went in to retrieve it.

"He's a minor," Miller said, coming back with my driver's license.

"Where are your parents?" Officer Albert asked.

"They're in New York for a family gathering at my grandparents' house."

"Do you know how to reach them?"

"No," I said, so dazed and confused from the beating I had just taken, I couldn't remember a thing. Then it came back to me.

"The phone number's in an address book in the kitchen."

Miller went back in to retrieve it.

"Justin," Officer Albert said. "I'd like to take your statement, but as a minor, we need to have an adult family member present. Are there any other members of your family around?"

Still in shock, I shook my head. I couldn't think of a thing.

"Oh yeah," I said, after a minute. "My other grandparents live nearby."

"Do you have their phone number?"

"It's in the address book, too."

When Miller came back with the address book, I showed them the two numbers.

"Okay," Trooper Albert said. "Let's try to call your parents first."

We went inside the house and Trooper Albert called my grandparents' home in New York.

"This is Trooper Albert with the State Police," he said when someone answered. "I need to speak with Mr. James Bailey, please."

Trooper Albert waited.

"Yes, hello, Mr. Bailey," he said. "This is Trooper Albert with the State Police. There's been a shooting here at your home and you need to come home right away."

There was a pause.

"I'm sorry, sir, but this isn't a practical joke. It's a serious matter. There's been a shooting at your residence involving your son and you need to return home immediately."

There was another pause.

"No, no, your son is alive, but I am unable to divulge any more information to you over the phone. How soon can you be back here?"

"About two hours? No, that will be fine. In the meantime, Justin has told us there's another set of grandparents nearby. Is that correct? Yes, uh huh. Well, we'll be attempting to unite Justin with your father and I would recommend you drive there upon returning to the neighborhood. Your home is now a crime scene and we'll have it cordoned off until at least sometime this afternoon. Yes, as I said, Justin is doing just fine for now."

Trooper Albert hung up and looked at me.

"Justin, where does your other grandfather live?"

"Off of Adams Road at Hardey's Lake."

"Okay, I'm going to try and get in touch with him now."

Again he dialed a number and waited. A few moments later someone answered.

"Mr. Bailey? Yes, this is Trooper Albert with the State Police. We have your grandson Justin here at his home and I need your presence immediately."

There was a pause.

"No, that's fine. I'll have one of our cruisers pick you up. Please just get dressed and be ready to leave. Yes. Thank you, I'll explain everything when you get here."

I was escorted back out to the police cruiser. Another cop came around with a Polaroid camera and took a half dozen photos of my face and body. I was asked for a profile from both sides. By that point, both of my eyes had nearly swollen shut. I was unable to breathe through my nose. My ears were black and blue and the back of my head was throbbing. There were flashing lights around us everywhere.

As I stood against the police cruiser, my grandfather came up the driveway. He seemed especially frail with his disheveled gray hair. He was wearing wire-framed glasses and his eyes were filled with tears. Trooper Albert took him aside and quietly explained what had happened.

My grandfather came back barely able to mask his sadness.

"Are you OK?" he asked me, starting to cry uncontrollably.

I broke down and wept as he held me. Until that point, I had been going through the motions, but in one instant the shock had suddenly worn off and everything hit me. Dickie was dead. I was responsible. The day was dawning and my troubles had just begun.

Eventually my grandfather held me back and looked into my eyes.

"Are you sure you're all right, Justin? You're all beaten up."

Trooper Albert came over to intervene.

"I'm going to request that we proceed over here next to the cabin so I can take Justin's statement."

Trooper Albert asked one question and jotted down the answer in his notebook. Then he asked another question and another. My grandfather kept his arm around me the entire time.

"Justin, is there anything else you can tell us about this incident?"

"No, sir. Not to my recollection."

"Very well. Why don't the two of you remain here next to the cabin and Mr. Bailey, as soon as I can, I'll get an officer to take you home."

We had been standing there for several minutes when I recognized that one of the police officers was this guy named Jimmy. We had ridden the bus to school together for a decade until he graduated a few years back. He came over.

"Hey, Justin," he said. "I'm really sorry this has happened to you."

"I didn't know you had become a police officer," I said.

"Yeah."

He stared at my face.

"Man, Dickie really beat you up good."

"Yeah. Is it bad?"

"Oh my God, Justin. Your entire face is black and blue. Even your ears. And your nose is all busted up, too."

"The back of my head really hurts. I think it's from Dickie banging it up against the front door."

"We should probably have you looked at before you go."

He left to find a paramedic. My grandfather squeezed his arm around me tighter. Jimmy came back with a paramedic who, a minute later, had looked me over.

"You should see a doctor when your parents get back," the paramedic said. "You may have a concussion. It's best to have it checked out within 24 hours."

Officer Miller came back just then and said he was ready to drive us over to my grandfather's place. With a line of cars filling the driveway, Miller led us down to the cruiser nearest the road. As we approached the police cruiser, Maria arrived with a friend. Maria got out of her car, looking shocked. My grandfather walked a short distance away to give us some privacy.

"What is going on, Justin? What are all these cop cars and ambulances doing here?"

"Didn't you hear?"

"No, what?"

"Dickie came here to attack me and I shot him. He's dead."

Maria screamed and became hysterical.

"All right, all right," the officer said. "I'm going to have to ask you to leave."

"Okay," Maria yelled. "But I just need to ask him one question." She looked back at me.

"Why, Justin? Why did you kill him?"

"Because he was going to kill me."

"Oh God. That was so wrong, Justin. God, I can't believe you did this."

"I can't believe it either. You're acting like I shot him in cold blood. I was defending my life, Maria! Don't you get it?! He was going to kill me."

Maria pulled away from me, still crying hysterically. I was crying, too. Maria's friend came over to comfort her.

"I'm sorry," Maria said finally. "But I can't be with you anymore. Not after what you did. You killed Dickie."

She and her friend started back toward Maria's car, but Officer Albert had heard the commotion and came down to intercept them.

"Are you Maria Gallo?"

"Yes," she said, with tears filling her eyes.

"Okay, I'll need for you to stay and make a statement."

Officer Miller opened the back door for my grandfather and me.

"Here's a jacket to cover your head," he said once we were all inside. "The media is already parked down on Quarry Road."

As he started down the road toward my grandfather's place, I looked back once at Maria. She hadn't bothered to look up. Her words weighed heavy on my heart. I was confused and filled with grief. Maria was my first love, my only love. I had built my entire world around her and now when I needed her most, she had abandoned me again.

My grandfather let me know when we had passed all the media and I pulled the jacket off my head. As the countryside passed by, I resolved to kill myself the first chance I got. I had nothing more to live for now. I had killed somebody I knew, and the love of my life had just told me goodbye for doing it. The first chance I got, I was putting a gun to my own head.

When we arrived at my grandparents' house, I curled up on a bed in a back bedroom and quickly passed out from exhaustion. When I awoke several hours later, my parents and my older brother Jacob were there. I explained again to everyone what had happened. As the horror and anguish of the whole episode returned, I cried uncontrollably again. Everyone cried with me. When I stopped, I touched my swollen face.

"It really hurts."

"Oh, honey. We need to take you to a doctor right away."

She looked at my dad.

"My God, he's so badly beaten up."

"How do you feel?" my father asked, trying to be the practical one.

"Awful. I'm so tired and confused."

He patted me on the shoulder.

"Go ahead and call," he said to Mom. "See what you can arrange."

My mother went to look up the number in the phonebook. I heard her making the call.

"I got a recording," she said, coming back. "They're closed until Monday."

"Maybe you should take him to the emergency room," my grandmother said.

"No, please. I don't want to go anywhere right now," I said. "Can't it just wait until Monday?"

"No it can't, Justin. You may have a concussion," my mother said.

"Well listen, let's just see how he feels this afternoon and tomorrow," Dad said. Looking at me he said, "If you're not showing any signs of improvement, we're going to have to get you some medical attention right away."

Things settled down into a state of quiet grief from there. I stared off into space, feeling numb. Everyone spoke in whispered voices around me.

At some point that afternoon, the police called to say it was all right for us to return home. I rode in the back of the car with a terrible headache. The horror of it all played over and over in my head.

We pulled up and found all the police cars and ambulances had gone, but the gathering of media trucks down at the bottom of our driveway had multiplied in their absence. My mother quickly covered me with her coat as we went past them. From the car, I was hurried into the house. We passed where Dickie had been shot along the way. I noticed there were still bits of his blood clotted up all over the driveway and patio. As soon as I was safely inside, my father went back outside and ran the hose until every bit of it was gone from sight.

My mother heated up some soup for me. After I had eaten, I went upstairs to sleep again. I slept through that night and well into the next day. When I awakened my mother was at my bedside.

"How are you feeling, honey?"

"I wanna die, Mom, I wanna die!"

I started to sob uncontrollably again.

"How can I go on anymore?! I killed somebody! Somebody with a mom and a dad and a family! I can't do it. I can't go on anymore. I wanna die."

"Don't say that, Sugarbear. Our life would be over without you!"

As she wept, I tried to dry my own tears.

"Oh, honey," she said. "I love you so much. Don't you know how much I love you? How...how...how much all of us love you!"

"But Mom, I can't live with this."

She shook me firmly.

"You are my life," she almost screamed. "OUR life! Please live if only for me...for us!"

She pulled my head up and made me look into her eyes. Her look in return was one that only a mother can give to her own child.

"Come downstairs, honey. I have something I want to show you."

Down on the first floor, I found the house packed with twenty or so of my relatives. Most of my aunts and my uncles had come, along with several of my cousins and my other grandparents. I broke down again at the sight of everyone. I had felt entirely alone and here everyone had come to offer their love and support. Some relatives had driven a few hundred miles to be there. My thoughts of killing myself slipped away. I was not alone in this world. My entire family would be there for me. If only for a little while, I was feeling comforted.

As I sat down and ate some breakfast, I became aware of the silence around me. The TV was off though I barely understood why. There would be an endless stream of chatter about the events of the previous day on the news.

The phone rang and my mother answered it.

"No," she said, several times. "No, out of respect for my son and the Hellerman family, we're not offering any more information."

She got off. The phone rang again almost immediately. It was someone else from the media. My mother gave them the same answer and hung up. She kept the cordless phone with her all day, fielding calls. Some were from friends, some from the parents of my classmates. There were even some from complete strangers, offering their support. My mother thanked each one in turn and said I wasn't taking calls.

I sat there mindlessly through it all. Members of my family kept patting me on the back.

"Hang in there, buddy. Everything will be okay."

I doubted that it ever would be okay. I was tortured by what had happened. It possessed my every thought. I had killed a fellow classmate, and the one person I really wanted around for comfort told me that she couldn't be with me anymore.

Eleven

Tiring of all the pats on the back and "chin up" stuff, I excused myself and went upstairs to lie on my bed. A few minutes later, my brother Jacob came up to see me.

"Hey, you okay, Justin?"

"Yeah, I'm just tired, Jacob."

He patted me on the shoulder and came over to sit next to me. I knew he was glancing at me out of the corner of his eye. A moment later, he tried to console me.

"Hey, remember that time when Dad had us snorkel all the way around Hardey's Lake?"

"Yeah," I said.

"Man we must have found a hundred or more fishing lures for Dad's tackle box that day. My fingers were like prunes by the time we got finished."

I had been staring at the ceiling and looked over at him.

"Look Jacob, I know you're trying to cheer me up, but I just want to be left alone for awhile. I need to sleep. Is that okay?"

"Yeah, yeah, sure, Justin. Hey, everything's going to be okay."

I nodded. He patted me on the shoulder again. Before going downstairs, he had another look around the room. "I love you, bro."

"I love you, too, Jacob."

As the time passed, I lay there listening to Mom answer the phone again and again. The subdued voices of my relatives were in the background.

At one point, I heard my mother answer the phone and say, "Hi, Ellen." My ears pricked up and I sat up in my bed. I knew it had to be Maria's mother. I heard the front door open and close and Mom's voice trailing off. I went to the stairwell and tried in vain to hear what she was saying.

When the front door reopened, I hopped back onto the bed.

"I'll call you and let you know," she said.

A few moments later, I heard footsteps coming up the stairs. My heart raced as my mother appeared at the top of the stairwell.

"I need to talk with you, honey, okay?"

"Sure, what's up?"

Mom came over and explained her conversation with Ellen. Apparently Maria felt awful about how she had reacted and wanted to see me again.

"How would you feel about going over to spend a few hours with Maria? I think she'd like that."

I began to cry. Thank God. I never thought that I would see Maria again.

Shortly afterward, we were off to Maria's house. As before, the road was a circus of media trucks and reporters so I hid under a blanket in back until we were well down the road and out of sight.

Ellen was outside when we arrived. She gave my mother a hug and a kiss and then hugged me extra long and whispered, "Justin, I'm so happy you're here." She had become like a second mother to me over the past year and I felt greatly comforted by her love and acceptance.

"Maria's inside," she said. "But I should warn you, she's been a complete wreck since she got back home. She blames herself for everything. Please go on in and see her. She's waiting for you in her bedroom."

Mom gave me another hug and I headed over to find Maria. She was lying on her bed in a fetal position, rocking back and forth and sobbing. When she saw me enter the room, we both lost it. I sat on Maria's bed and we cried together.

"I'm so sorry, Justin. I just didn't know how to make sense of things earlier."

I kissed her on her forehead and held her in silence as tears flowed from our eyes.

"This is my fault, Justin," she cried.

"No it's not, honey. Please don't say that, okay?"

"I just don't know what to do."

"Me neither, Maria."

My mother came in with Ellen a short while later and joined in the hug fest. All of us were on the bed, sobbing uncontrollably. I looked up and noticed Nick and the kids just outside of the door. They were crying, too.

Eventually everyone agreed it was best to go to the kitchen. Nick gave me a big hug out in the hallway.

"Hey, partner. I know this is going to be tough for awhile, but you come around here anytime you want."

He nodded at my mother.

"Just consider this his second home."

He looked back at me.

"All right, Justin?"

I nodded.

"Hey, it's summertime. We'll do our best to forget this situation and have some fun."

"Thanks," I said. I could not imagine forgetting what had happened but it meant the world to me to have Maria and her family in my corner.

Nick hugged me again and fought back his own tears. The young kids grabbed hold of me too, and everyone started crying again.

Finally we got ourselves over to the kitchen and sat around drinking iced tea and talking. Maria and I went to sit outside. The air was perfectly warm that day. The lake was sparkling in the sun. It was hard to see through the sorrow and shock at that point. I still sat there wishing I could go back in time and change everything, but just being out in the fresh summer air seemed to clear my mind just a bit.

Mom eventually took me home. The weekend seemed to drag on forever. I heard all sorts of reports about Dickie's death on the news. A lot of it was inaccurate. Several newspapers and television stations had portrayed their version of the incident. The press in general only got one part of the story, Dickie was dead and I killed him. Again and again I lived through the horror of that fateful morning in my own mind.

My brother left to go back to college on Sunday afternoon. Most of my other relatives left as well. Donnie called to see how I was doing after dinner.

"I drove by, thinking to say hello, but it's a total zoo down on the road."

"I know. I have to hide every time we come and go."

"Did you hear about the meeting at the school?"

"No," I said. "What meeting?"

"They brought in these counselors at school to offer grief management and stuff. A bunch of students came in and they had a big meeting in the auditorium. The news people were out there interviewing us as we went by."

"Did they interview you?"

"No, but they interviewed a couple of Dickie's friends. You

should have heard them. 'Dickie was such a nice guy. I've known him forever. I can't believe this has happened.' Someone even said they would gladly have gotten in the way of the bullet for Dickie. What a joke."

"How about everybody else?" I asked. "Does everybody hate me and feel sorry for Dickie or what?"

"No, man. Well, you know, some people were his friends and would defend him no matter what, but mostly people are just sad and mixed up. I saw a lot of people crying out in the parking lot."

I sat there in silence, not knowing what else to say.

"Hey, don't let it get you down," Donnie said.

"Yeah, I'm trying not to. It's just really hard."

There was silence again.

"Hey, you want me to come over and hang with you a bit?"

"Yeah, you really can't though. My parents want to keep things as quiet as possible for now. You know, with the press and everything. I think we're going to see an attorney tomorrow."

"Yeah? All right. Well, everybody's behind you, man and, you know, if you need any moral support, just let me know. I'm there for you. We'd all like to come and see you."

"Thanks. I'm sure I'll see you soon."

I got calls from all my friends in the junior and senior class. The conversations went mostly along the same lines. I explained again what had happened. We'd cry and talk for a while and say goodbye. Then I'd go back up to the darkness of my room.

On Monday morning, my parents took me to the doctor's office to be checked out. I was asked a multitude of questions and the doctor ran some tests. He came back into the examination room a short while later.

"It's very possible that Justin received a concussion from the blows to his face and head. It's also very possible that if the beating had continued, he would have been left a vegetable or with permanent brain damage."

Afterward my parents took me to see an attorney. His name was Bruno Russell. We listened as he explained the range of possible charges I might face, which included anything from murder to voluntary manslaughter to involuntary manslaughter to aggravated assault to nothing at all. The district attorney had to decide one way or the other in the next few days.

Either way, the legal process would be slow, but Bruno assured us that he could arrange for me to remain in the care of my parents until the trial was over. He seemed very confident that I would be exonerated. It was good to hear that, but even the slimmest possibility of being imprisoned left me feeling sick to my stomach.

The hours and minutes of that week passed by interminably. I was waiting to learn what charges would be filed against me. The circus of reporters never left the road down below. The story seemed like it was on the news night and day.

I was at home one afternoon listening to a report when the word got out. I had been charged with voluntary and involuntary manslaughter. The court date was set for December. That meant I would be going to court in the middle of my senior year. I stood watching the TV in disbelief. I had begun to think that I wouldn't be charged at all.

With the memory of Dickie's death like a poisoned fog around our house, my parents considered selling the place, but my father said we were too strapped to move. Besides, he loved the seclusion of the woods and so did everyone else in the family.

The events of that terrible morning stayed with me everywhere I went. It was especially vivid each time I looked in the mirror and saw the bruises on my face and head. Slowly they healed but the memories continued to haunt me.

I spent much of the summer over at Maria's place. With the lake and the swimming pool and all the other stuff, there was always something to take my mind off of the tragedy, although it was impossible to forget it entirely. Ellen took time off from work and did her best to help. She arranged lots of fun in the sun and Nick made sure no one got on his property to bother us.

Toward the end of the summer, Maria made a decision to attend a college a few miles away from our high school. I was thrilled with her choice because it meant we would still be together. We had become inseparable over the summer and her companionship was absolutely necessary to me.

With the start of school right around the corner, the specter of being confronted by hundreds of students and teachers was rapidly approaching. Some of them would be my allies, some would rather see me dead. I had been protected from encounters with people in town for the most part, but on the few occasions we had gone out in public, there were looks and there were whispers. There was a feeling of gossip and judgment in the air.

The week before school began, Maria's parents took us out to the fall fair. It was an hour's drive away and the first time Maria and I had felt free to be ourselves in public since the shooting. We were far enough away from home that no one knew us. There were no fingers being pointed or whispers as Maria and I walked through the crowd hand in hand.

I bought Maria a piece of pizza first thing and took her on the Ferris wheel, then tried to win her a big teddy bear. It felt so great to be normal, even if just for a brief afternoon. It was such simple pleasure to eat cotton candy and take carnival rides and go about my life without it being a tragedy.

As I walked up to school on the first day back, I was filled with anxiety about how I would be received. As I had feared, there were silent stares and a sense that people were purposely ignoring me. My thought was to run away, but eventually someone came up and patted me on the back, and then another person did, and by the end of the day, I felt that most of the school was behind me. There were hateful stares from Dickie's staunchest allies, but by and large, everyone made me feel welcome and I mostly felt at peace being there at school.

One big exception was my old friend Crystal. I walked into our art class that first afternoon and saw her sitting by the window. I went over to say hello and she turned away from me. We had been friends since we were little kids, yet she went about organizing her table as if I weren't there. I went back to my table, crushed by the rejection. I had never judged her for trying to bang every football player in my parents' bedroom or throwing up in their bed. I guess it was a reminder that things may be unpredictable. It was also a reminder of how things would never be the same in my life and I would never be the same person I once was.

Sometime later in my chemistry lab, Mark, Troy and Jon started busting my chops about running for class president again.

"Just like last year," Mark said. "You know, you'll promise everyone chicks and booze and, what else…"

"Three-day school weeks," Troy chimed in.

"Yeah," Mark said. "And everyone will vote for you."

I shook my head, thinking it was a lousy idea. Yeah, most of the students had shown their support for me, but the last thing I needed was to be in the spotlight.

"Come on," Jon said.

"I don't know."

"Come on. We'll totally be behind you. We'll make it a blast."

After a lot of prodding and arm-twisting, I reluctantly acquiesced and sat down with them and put together my speech.

The main idea was, every time I offered one of my power points, my friends would jump up in the front row and give me a standing ovation. We laughed hysterically. It was nice to feel normal again.

When Crystal decided to run against me, I panicked and almost changed my mind. As the campaign unfolded, her hatred for me became more venomous. I never learned the reasons behind her resentments but suspected that maybe she and Dickie had been having a secret affair or something. Either way, I finally got upset and let out my own resentments in the campaign. I was gonna be strong and not let her pettiness get to me.

The day we gave our speeches in the school auditorium, I stood up in front of my fellow classmates and went down the laundry list of things I was going to do for them that Crystal could not. I made all sorts of extravagant promises, and after each one of them, my friends stood up in the front row and made a bunch of noise as promised. This elicited a similar response from most of my other classmates.

"So remember, when you are placing your vote, I'm Justin Bailey."

I pointed a finger at Crystal.

"And SHE'S NOT!" I exclaimed, letting out weeks of frustration.

The whole auditorium erupted. Everyone stood up to applaud. I raised my hands up in a "V." My friends started to chant and clap. "Vote for!" clap, clap "Justin Bailey!" "Vote for!" clap, clap "Justin Bailey!" "Vote for!" clap, clap "Justin Bailey!"

I raised my hands in the air again and basked in the adulation. Crystal seethed. Two days later, I learned that I had won in another landslide. Crystal received only a few votes. I had ambivalent feelings about beating her so badly. It was wonderful to be accepted by my entire class, but each time I crossed paths with Crystal now, I could see how her hatred for me had only been magnified. Any hope of our being friends again had been extinguished. I didn't need people in my life like her, anyway.

With the election over, I immersed myself in my studies and time with friends to forget. My English class with Mrs. Walden was one of my sanctuaries. This short woman with the luxurious brown hair and sparkling eyes stirred my interest in literature and made me feel like family in her class. Talking about the stories we read was like sitting around the table with Mark Twain while he filled your mind with dreams of great adventure.

My other favorite classes were art with Mr. Darby and drama with Mrs. Collins. Mr. Darby always dressed very dapperly and made his art class lots of fun. He was extremely flamboyant and hysterical to be around. Mostly we socialized and goofed off and had fun with friends. Mr. Darby did cool things like bring in a small single burner stove and cooked artichokes in class.

Crystal was in both my art and drama classes. Having two classes a day with her was definitely awkward and distressing at first. In fact, the only downer about drama class was Crystal, but on the other hand I loved the funny skits and different exercises we did so much, it hardly mattered. I ignored Crystal and she pretended like I did not exist.

The court proceedings began shortly before Christmas. We arrived at the courthouse that first day, confronted by another media horde. There was a large group, a dozen strong, of the Hellerman family in front of the building. They stared with hatred as we pushed through the crowd behind our attorney.

I got a sick feeling the minute I saw the judge. He was somebody's bad idea of a Midwestern schoolteacher; small, stern, gray-haired with wire-framed glasses and never a smile.

District Attorney Johnson tried to come off like he was a star on one of those primetime legal dramas, but with his cheap suit, thick prescription glasses and hair poorly parted to one side, he would have been more at home in a comedy skit. If not for the fact that he was intent on convicting me of the maximum possible charges, his appearance would have been comical.

On that first day, I saw the DA get approving glances from the Hellerman family. My family got icy stares. It dawned on me that, for all intents and purposes, Johnson was like their attorney.

Juveniles had to be tried by a judge and I learned there would be no jury. I took another long look at Judge Murkowski and again felt sick in my gut. My fate was in his hands, and judging from his demeanor, he didn't seem like the person I wanted for that job.

Out of curiosity at one point, I glanced back at the gallery and found the Hellerman family glaring my way. It was clear that hatred would be boring into my back all day long every day. I quickly looked forward again. It was hard to imagine weeks and months of enduring their embittered stares, but all I could do was face forward, avoid eye contact, and ignore them as much as possible.

After being arraigned on voluntary and involuntary manslaughter charges, my status as a student was discussed. The judge deferred to Bruno and school officials on this point and said he would schedule the trial at most for two or three days each week, depending on the witnesses and evidence. I would be excused from my classes on those days and was to attend school on all the others.

The judge scheduled the actual trial to resume in January and ordered me to have a psychological evaluation in the meantime. The particulars of the evaluation were discussed and court adjourned.

Outside the courtroom, Bruno again helped our family make our way through the crush of media. My family steered clear of communicating with them, feeling it was the best way to deal with it out of respect for the Hellerman family. The Hellermans had quickly gathered out there and met us with their cold glares. The press kept badgering us for some comment but we climbed into our car without offering any kind of statement. Before we drove off, I heard Roy Hellerman scream into the bank of microphones.

"This kid murdered my son and we're not gonna let him get away with it!"

I went home feeling depressed. I had hated one day of the proceedings and had an endless procession of them waiting ahead of me.

I lay in bed, beating myself up again over what I had done. I could not keep myself from going over that entire event. I wanted to think that I would have done the same thing, given the same scenario, but who knew? My mind went around and around and came back to the same simple fact. I had killed someone's son, someone's brother and friend and that idea drove me back into depression.

I called and sought comfort from Maria.

"Did you want to come over?" she asked.

"I can't. My parents said it was best if I didn't go anywhere tonight."

"Maybe tomorrow then?"

"Yeah, maybe tomorrow."

"Did you want to talk about it?"

I told her about feeling depressed.

"I can't imagine what you're feeling," Maria said. "But that's why the law allows for self-defense, I think. Dickie didn't have to come stalking you at your house. It was his choice. Remember, he was following us around and bullying you that entire evening. He just wanted trouble and that's it."

"Yeah."

"Yeah, it's not your fault, Justin."

"I guess."

"It's not!"

"But you know what else bothers me?"

"What?"

"I have to be in the same courtroom almost every day of the week with Dickie's entire family and let me tell you, if looks could kill, Maria, I would be dead by now. The last time I saw looks of hate that awful was from Dickie when I called him a drunken bum."

"It's going be tough, but you've got to be strong, babe."

"I know." There was a long pause. "I love you."

"I love you, too. Come over tomorrow night, okay? We'll spend quality time together."

"Okay."

"I'll make you dinner."

"Yeah, that sounds good. I love you."

"I love you, too."

"Hey, my mom's calling me for something. I've got to go."

I took the phone and went downstairs to wash up.

Eli called a short while after dinner. I took the phone out to the front porch. It was a cold night. The pines looked frozen with winter.

"Dude," Eli said. "You're all over the news tonight."

"I know."

I watched my breath in the cold air.

"So, how did it go?"

"Truth be told, it sucked."

I explained about the Hellerman family, the judge and the prosecutor.

"The judge is like the guy who yells at the neighborhood kids for playing on his lawn. The DA is the biggest loser. Like his socks don't match and his glasses are held together with electrical tape, but he thinks he's cool."

Eli laughed.

"So, what's next?"

"I don't have to go back to court until after the holidays. I guess there's another day of arguing between our attorney and the DA before the trial actually starts, but it's all a mystery to me. I'll tell you this much, it's not like Perry Mason, that's for sure."

"That's funny. So, you'll be at school tomorrow?"

"Yeah."

"I can't believe it's almost Christmas."

I glanced inside at our Christmas tree all lit up. I thought of Dickie's family and how hard it would be for them around the holiday season.

"So," Eli said. "Can you hang out with us this weekend or what?"

"I'm not sure. I'll have to check with my mom but I doubt it."

"Okay, well, we'll see you at school tomorrow. You're going to be like a celebrity."

"No, I don't want to be a celebrity. Not like this."

"Okay, well, we'll just go to our classes and stuff and act like none of this ever happened."

"Yeah, good idea. Hey man, I'll see you tomorrow," I said.

"Okay, don't let it get you down. You know all your friends are behind you."

"I know. Thanks."

I got off and went back inside. My parents were usually watching TV about this time but it was off and they were reading, my father a *Field & Stream* magazine, my mother a "how to" book on crocheting or something.

"Guess I'll go do my homework," I said and started upstairs.

"Okay, Sugarbear," Mom said. "Don't worry. Everything will be all right. Good night. I love you."

"Yeah, good night," my father said. "I love you, too."

I nodded and went up to my room.

The next day at school, I found my life had become even more dramatic. It felt like there was a buzz about the trial all up and down the hallways. Then I walked in and all fell silent. There were smiles, a few words of encouragement, and a lot of uncomfortable looks. No one wanted to say anything directly to my face. All I could think about was how glad I would be for the final day of school and the start of Christmas break.

I started over to Maria's place that night excited at the prospect of seeing her. Her home continued to be a place of sanctuary for me. There was always something going on that helped me to forget.

Along the way, I stopped for gas and decided to go in for a soda. While I looked in the cooler, I heard someone whisper up front.

"That's the shooter."

Out of the corner of my eye, I saw it was an older couple. They paid for their stuff and left. I went up to the register and pretended not to have heard anything.

"You done with the gas?" the checker said.

I looked out at the pump. It had stopped at full. I noticed the old couple looking at me as they pulled away.

"Yeah," I said to the checker.

He took my money and gave me the change. I walked out feeling depressed. That was my life. One minute I was up. The next minute I was down, my feelings of joy fleeting, carried away by a fresh round of paranoia, fear, or rejection. I was always hearing someone whisper behind my back. The press referred to me as "the shooter." I'm sure a lot of people in town did the same. A normal life was impossible. I started the car and hurried on my way. With my luck I'd run into one of the Hellerman kids next.

At Maria's place, I parked in the driveway and went up to the door, feeling crappy. She opened it before I could knock and gave me a big hug.

"Aren't you glad to see me?" she asked.

"Yeah, yeah. I'm just kind of feeling down right now."

"Why? What happened?"

"Oh, not much. It's just that everybody I come across hates me or something."

She gave me another hug.

"Come on in. I've got some news that will really cheer you up."

"Good, because finding out that my nickname is now "the shooter" is really bumming me out."

Maria gave me a kiss and we walked to the kitchen where I was greeted by Ellen and Nick.

"Hey, why the long face?" Ellen asked when I walked in.

"Just one of those days, I guess."

"Well did Maria tell you the good news?"

I sat down next to Maria and waited to hear what was next.

"Go ahead, Mom, you tell him," Maria said.

"What?" I asked.

Ellen uncovered some paperwork on the kitchen table. There were several travel brochures and what looked like airline tickets.

"How would you like to go down to an amusement park in Florida with us over the holidays?"

"Well it's more like a vacation resort," Nick said.

I looked at Maria. She had a big, glowing smile on her face. I looked back at Ellen.

"You're kidding, right?"

"Not a bit, sweety. We've got it all planned. Check it out."

She opened one of the brochures and started talking about the place where we would stay. I looked quickly over at Maria. She could barely contain her excitement and came to lean against my shoulder.

"Check out this white sandy beach," Ellen said. "Does that look beautiful or what?"

"Man, I can't even believe we're talking about this. Are you serious?"

"Totally serious. All you have to do is say yes."

I was overcome with emotion. Maria squeezed me tightly.

"Hey, hey," Nick said. "This is supposed to be a happy occasion."

Lost in emotion, I leapt up and gave Nick and Ellen a big hug. Ellen held me back and looked into my eyes.

"We know how tough things have been for you guys. You can't turn around in this little town without it being in your face, so we figured, let's get out of town for a week or so. What do you say? We can all just be ourselves without all the stress for a spell."

"Oh man, I'd love to."

"Doesn't it sound cool?" Maria asked.

She jumped up and down.

Ellen smiled, gave me another hug and went back to cooking dinner. I called home and my mother confirmed that it was all right for me to go.

"Are you sure you don't mind, Mom? I mean with it being Christmas and my birthday and everything?"

"No, not at all. It'll be good for you to get away, I think."

I got off the phone, my head in a cloud. The kids came downstairs to eat and all we did was talk about the trip the entire meal. Afterward, Maria and I took the brochures into her room.

"Wow, I still can't believe this is happening," I said.

Maria plopped on the bed with me.

"The only place I've ever been to on vacation is in Ocean City, Maryland."

"Well is it fun there, too?"

"Yeah, I guess. We usually camp outside in tents."

"Are you serious? You stayed near the beach in tents."

"Yeah, it was actually kind of cool. Except for the days when it would rain."

Maria giggled.

"This is going to be the best vacation ever!"

Twelve

A few days before Christmas, we drove to the airport. It was a cold, miserable day as we boarded the plane. We landed in Florida under balmy blue skies.

There was excitement in everything we did -- picking up the car at the airport, arriving to the vacation resort, walking into the tropical décor of our hotel lobby. We were surrounded by dark wood, bamboo, palms and staff dressed like Polynesians. There was a feeling we had crossed the Seven Seas. I felt like a kid again.

Maria and I took the keys and went running up ahead with the kids to the room. It had the same décor as the lobby, only in lighter colors. A big sliding glass door led out to a balcony. The balcony overlooked a lagoon. The lagoon was totally beautiful and had the whitest sand I had ever seen. The kids were jumping around as Nick and Ellen came in with the bellboy.

"Check it out," Maria said.

Ellen joined us out on the balcony. Nick tipped the bellboy and opened the door to the other room of the suite. Maria and I joined him to have a look.

"Cool, huh?" he said, then in a whisper. "The kids are sleeping here. I got you and Maria your own room next door."

Maria grabbed the keys with excitement.

"No way, are you kidding me."

"Well you guys deserve it," Ellen said.

"Thank you," I said.

"Hey, why doesn't everyone change and get comfortable," Ellen said. She looked at her watch. "Then we can meet back here in fifteen minutes and go downstairs for lunch."

Maria and I went to our room with our luggage. As soon as the door closed, she dragged me onto the bed and started kissing me.

"This is so great," she said.

"Yeah, I never want to leave."

We both changed our clothes and hurried down to meet the others. Everyone had gotten into their swimsuits and flip flops.

The décor of the restaurant was just as beautiful as the lobby and our rooms. All the waitresses were dressed like hula girls. Tropical music played in the background. There were palm trees and carved wooden faces at every turn. It was easy to get enchanted by it all.

After lunch, we went down to lounge at the beach. Nick and Ellen ordered some tropical cocktails with little umbrellas in them. We talked about all the places we were going to visit. We were going to see every theme park there was to see in the resort.

The next day was Christmas Eve and everything was especially festive around the place. We ate at this neat little restaurant that was done up just like a page out of the brochure and then went on our way. We spent the day enjoying the scenery, shopping around and riding as many rides as possible.

"I can't believe there's so much to do," I said, flopping onto our bed at the end of the day.

"I know," Maria said, lying next to me.

She looked into my eyes.

"Let's just get jobs down here and never go back."

I looked away.

"I wish."

"Oh, it will be all right," she said.

"I hope so. I think that one minute. Then I feel like it's just wishful thinking."

I looked back at her.

"I kind of go around and around like that all day long."

"Let's just enjoy ourselves while we're here, okay, honey?"

"Yeah, you're right."

"I can't wait to get up tomorrow."

Maria opened the sliding door to the balmy breeze and we fell asleep to the sound of the rustling palm trees and a gentle summer wind.

On Christmas morning we had breakfast in one of the other restaurants. There was a great deal of excited chatter around the table about our plans for the day. In the end we agreed that we would lie around on the beach under the umbrellas until early afternoon, have lunch, then shower and head out for the night.

While we were lying there by the blue water after breakfast, Ellen suggested that I call my folks.

As I got up, Maria started to pack up her stuff as well.

"Yeah, I feel like cleaning up a bit, too," Maria said. "I'll come with you."

We headed back to our room. I called my parents and talked with them for about a half an hour. Apparently it had snowed there on Christmas Eve. They couldn't believe we were wearing swimsuits and lounging around under palm trees.

If I felt down at all after getting off the phone, there was little time to mope. Marias' parents arranged for us to attend the Christmas Day parade nearby. There was another big rush as everyone got dressed and within the hour we were watching the parade and waving to all the cartoon characters.

On our final day, Nick arranged for us to have a special dinner, both in honor of New Year's Eve and my birthday, which was on New Year's Day. At midnight, everyone sang "Happy Birthday" to me and we watched the most amazing fireworks show ever. I was kind of sad going back to the hotel, realizing that we had to leave the next day.

For over a week I'd almost entirely forgotten about Dickie, his family, and my trial but soon the nightmare would be back. I would be returning to face the same dismal existence I had left behind just a week earlier. Maria was chirping away about all our adventures on our flight home but I kept staring out the window, thinking of all the horrible things to come.

Thirteen

A week after our return, I was back in court. Bruno argued with the DA over what evidence was admissible and what wasn't, who would be called to testify and who wouldn't. My parents were among those scheduled to take the stand. So were Maria, State Trooper Albert, the coroner, Bill Simpson, the friend who had given Dickie a ride over to my house, and John Walters, one of Dickie's neighbors. Most of the other people called to the stand were there to provide some kind of expert testimony or to serve as a character witness.

The next day of the trial was scheduled for the following month. I lay awake late that night, thinking and worrying about what lay ahead and also wondering about the psychiatric evaluation scheduled for the following day. I had no idea what to expect, only that the evaluation was to be done at a place called the Catholic Social Services in the city. The city was about a 40-minute drive from our home.

My mother took me to the appointment in the morning. We sat waiting in a reception room for fifteen minutes. Finally a man in a nice suit came out to greet us.

"Hi. I'm Fred Delano."

He shook hands, first with my mother, then with me. Dr. Delano was a right around six feet tall with the build of a man who spent more time in his head than in his body. He wasn't fat but he definitely wasn't athletic. He wore wire-rimmed glasses, his dark hair was receding, and he had a full beard.

All in all, he seemed like a very nice man.

"Mrs. Bailey, I trust the court explained that I would be evaluating Justin alone today."

"I understand," she said. "But someone had to drive him here, so hopefully you don't mind my waiting."

"No, no, not at all. I was only thinking, perhaps you'd like to go shopping for an hour or so, rather than sitting here alone and waiting."

"No, it's fine. It looks like you have an abundance of magazines to read."

Dr. Delano smiled.

"And again, you're completely welcome. I'll try to move along through the evaluation as quickly as I can."

He smiled again and turned to me.

"Justin. Shall we?"

I looked back once as Dr. Delano closed his office door. My mom smiled. He invited me to sit at his desk and went around to sit on the other side and smiled.

"So, Justin, how much did the court explain to you about this evaluation process?"

"Not much. Only that we had to come."

"Well, just so you know, you'll be returning here at least two times, maybe three, in order for me to complete the evaluation. I hope you don't mind."

"No."

"Are you uncomfortable?"

"A little."

"Well don't be, Justin. The court just wants me to find out if you're crazy or not."

I giggled at hearing this. He grinned from ear to ear.

"Seriously though, we need to do a thorough evaluation of your state of mind regarding this incident, after which I will submit my findings to the court in writing."

I looked down.

"Don't worry. I'm sure you'll be fine."

I looked up and sighed nervously.

"Listen, I know this is anything but pleasant for you, but just pretend I'm your best friend and you've been dying to get everything off your chest. Okay?"

I nodded.

"So, go ahead and tell me your story. You can start wherever you like."

For well over an hour, I recounted how I had come to know Dickie and the way he had bullied and harassed me and how everything led to his coming to beat me up at my house. Dr. Delano took notes and occasionally interrupted me to clarify some things. By the end, I was crying. Dr. Delano passed me a box of tissues. When I had calmed down a bit, he spoke.

"Justin, let's try to put this in a bit of perspective. We're creatures, animals still, really. If you were a primitive man and a wild beast came at you, you'd defend yourself, right?"

"Yeah, I guess so."

"Well, it was that or get eaten by a saber-toothed tiger. Or run really fast."

I smiled.

"My point is, these instincts are ancient in us. You were attacked. It was only natural to defend yourself. Of course there were other responses you might have had. Running away, for instance, or calling the police, but we do the best we can under extreme circumstances as these. Planning to kill someone is one thing. Killing someone under duress is another thing altogether and I can assure you right now, you're not a cold-hearted killer, Justin. You just instinctively defended your life."

He came around and patted me on the shoulder.

"Let's go out and find out how many magazines your mother has been through while we've been talking."

He opened the door for me and followed me out.

"You have a fine young son here, Mrs. Bailey," he said.

She smiled and hugged me close with one arm.

"Now, as I was explaining to Justin, I'll need to see him again two or three more times, so why don't you folks go home, look at your schedule and call back to let us know when it would be convenient for the next appointment. I'd like to give it at least a few days between each one, so maybe next week?"

"That's fine," my mother said.

"Not too much longer. I don't want to leave too much time between sessions, either. Oh, and you'll need to call these folks over at social services to arrange some testing for Justin."

Dr. Delano handed my mother a card.

"They'll explain everything when you get there but just think of it as a complement to what we're doing here. Don't worry. It's no big deal."

"Thank you," my mother said and put the card away.

Dr. Delano shook hands with her and me and went back into his office.

"Let's go get something to eat," Mom said on the way out to the car.

Wrestling season had begun a week earlier and on the following Monday we had our first match. It was a home meet and our announcer made a big deal out of introducing our team over the loud speaker.

"And now the number one team in the district, the CASTLE STONE BLACK STALLIONS!!"

The home crowd went wild.

As was typical, both teams took five minutes to stretch, then all of the wrestlers lined up opposite their opponents on the wrestling mat. Each of them was introduced. Then it was my turn.

"Next, at 120 pounds, wrestling for Springville is Jim Taylor."

There was modest applause and some boos. Then I was introduced.

"At 120 pounds, for Castle Stone, Justin Bailey."

The crowd went wild. I looked up into the stands packed with students, teachers, family members and kids, taking in the adulation. Then I saw Roy Hellerman Jr. and my heart sank. The old terror returned. He was up in the stands with two of his friends. Roy Jr. had graduated from the same school in 1985, so I saw no reason for him to be there other than to hassle me, and that was how I felt. Roy was tall and thin and had the same seething stare as the rest of the family.

The coach came around telling everyone to get ready for the match. My teammates were jumping rope and stretching around the wrestling mat. There was the usual jock stuff going on to get ourselves psyched up.

I looked back up in the stands, I couldn't stop myself. Roy was still staring at me with his bloodless, pale blue eyes. His friends were staring, too. Not once did they look away at the other action around the gym.

As mine was one of the first matches on the schedule, my teammates started psyching me up.

"C'mon dude, kick this guy's ass. You got this, man!"

Ethan came over and massaged my shoulders.

"Come on, dude. Relax."

But I couldn't. With Dickie's big brother up there staring at me, it was like being hassled by Dickie all over again.

When my name was called, I snapped on my headgear, pulled up my knee pads and ran out to meet my opponent at center mat. We shook hands and the match began. Totally distracted by Roy Jr., I was immediately taken down. That focused me. All I needed was Roy up there gloating while I got my ass kicked. Focused now, I redoubled my efforts and squeaked out a win. Our team as a whole beat the crap out of Springville.

When I left to shower after the match, I saw Roy and his buddies staring back at me as they left the gym. I could tell that Dickie's brother was not going to let this go.

Back at home, my mother informed me that she had talked to the social services people and that we had been directed to a place called St. Mark's for the additional evaluation Dr. Delano had ordered.

"What's there?" I asked.

"I don't know, Sugarbear," my mother said. "All I know is it's up in Greenfield somewhere."

"So when are we supposed to go?"

"I set it up for tomorrow. And I made that second appointment with Dr. Delano for Thursday. The court wants this evaluation done before we meet him again."

I sat down, feeling depressed.

"Oh, don't make too much of it, honey. I'll be with you. And we'll go have ourselves an ice cream or something when we're done."

When we pulled up to the facility the next day, I felt my ears turn red. A sign on the brick building said, St. Mark's Juvenile Detention Center.

"You didn't say it was a juvenile detention center."

"Well, I didn't know, honey, but don't worry. I'm sure it's just a matter of convenience. What do you think, I'm going to leave you here?"

"Maybe."

She tussled my hair playfully but I wasn't amused. I was even less amused when we went inside. The place was dark and dingy-looking and smelled like an old dirty sock. The mood of the staff was grim. A woman wearing a uniform curtly informed my mother that she would have to wait in the lobby. She gave me a big hug and sat down. The woman instructed me to follow her. She started down a long hallway with a folder in her hand. Following along, I felt my chest tightening up with fear. How long was I supposed to be here? The woman had said the testing would take a few hours. I pictured myself never getting out of the place again.

I followed the woman down several hallways, up a flight of stairs and then down more hallways. We passed kids locked up behind bars along the way. Some were as young as eight or nine. None was older than I.

"Hey, who are you?" the inmates kept asking me as we passed along. "Why are you here, man? Are you new?"

I kept my mouth shut. The woman told the inmates to shut up and leave me alone.

Finally we entered a large room. It was empty except for two long cafeteria tables and some equipment on the tables that was not familiar to me. The walls were bare and painted a pure white. The floor was hardwood, like a basketball court, but not nearly as well polished.

I sat down. The technician hooked me up to an electronic device and the woman started to perform a series of tests. First she held up cards with ink blots on them and asked me to tell her what I saw. Then she asked me a series of questions.

"Do you think about hurting yourself? Do you think about hurting small animals?"

She was taking notes the entire time.

As the time went by, I became more stressed out. No one had explained the many procedures involved. I had no idea what would happen next or when it would be over.

Finally, after several hours, the woman walked me back out to the front lobby. My mother gave me a hug.

"There you are," she said, happy to see me.

"I'll be submitting these findings to Dr. Fred Delano," the woman said. "You're free to go now."

"That was a long time," Mom whispered as we headed for the door. "What on earth were they doing?"

"A bunch of weird stuff."

We stepped out into the sunlight as I explained.

"God, I am so glad to get out of there."

"Well, I have to admit," she said, "the place gave me the creeps, too."

"I wasn't sure they were going to let me leave."

"Oh, I would have come to rescue you, Sugarbear."

She patted my head.

"Stop it," I said.

"So, are you ready for that ice cream?"

"Yeah, and maybe something for lunch, too? I'm starved after being trapped inside that place."

"It was a crappy joint," Mom said. "Wasn't it?"

We both laughed and I told her about everything that happened as we drove along.

The next day we had the trial again and most of it was taken up by expert testimony. Eventually the coroner took the stand. You wouldn't think they could make that much out of the gun and the bullets and the blood, but they did. We were astonished when, during Bruno's cross-examination, it was brought to light that Dickie's blood alcohol level was nearly twice the legal limit and there were traces of marijuana and cocaine in his system.

It was hard to ignore the grief. Person after person came in to testify. Every little detail of evidence was discussed, reminding me constantly of the horror of that night.

All the while, Mr. and Mrs. Hellerman sat there, staring at me with hatred. Dickie was dead and I had pulled the trigger. Everyone knew that much. The question was, had I acted in self-defense? In my heart I was sure it was true. I also felt terrible for killing Dickie, but my remorse did not register with the Hellermans.

Later on that week we went back to see Dr. Delano again.

"So, Justin, how did you like St. Mark's Juvenile Detention Center?"

"I was totally freaked out the minute I walked in there."

Dr. Delano was reading through the evaluation they had sent over to him. He looked up over his glasses.

"So, I take it you're not up for a long-term visit."

I got a sick look on my face and he smiled.

"If you're wondering, the state requires multiple voices in this kind of evaluation and St. Mark's just happens to be the closest place with the proper testing equipment. There was no intent on my part to give you a heart attack."

"Well you did a pretty good job of it, intentionally or not."

Dr. Delano laughed and set down the report.

"Well, for the purposes of this session, I'd like you to make yourself comfortable on the couch while I'll ask you a series of questions."

I did as he had directed and described my feelings one more

time, before, during and after the shooting, plus my feelings about the trial itself, my hopes, expectations and fears about the outcome. He took notes as I spoke. When I described the prosecutor, Dr. Delano listened intently.

"Please tell me more," he said.

"Well, that guy just seems like he hates me as much as the Hellerman family."

"Just remember he's only doing his job."

"I know."

"Are you scared, Justin?"

"Yeah, like all the time."

"Okay, well let's talk about that."

After an hour, Dr. Delano set his notepad down.

"So, what do you think?" I asked.

"You mean, are you crazy?"

"Yeah."

"Oh, definitely. Certifiably nuts."

"No, seriously."

"Well, no. I think you're a completely normal young man, Justin."

"Is that good or bad."

He laughed.

"I mean for the trial."

"Well, let me put it this way. If the court thought you were mentally imbalanced, they could put you in a funny farm for a long, long time. And I don't think you'd particularly like that, Justin. But unless I find you're a danger to society in general, my opinion has no bearing on the verdict in your trial."

He saw my look of concern.

"Look, Justin. No one should give you false hopes, but even if you were convicted, which I personally don't think you will be, once they take into consideration your age, your otherwise responsible behavior and the special circumstances surrounding your case, you're likely to be looking at a matter of months behind barsn if that."

I was not much comforted and he saw that.

"Let me put it another way, Justin. People every day, everywhere face a measure of uncertainty in their lives and the only way to deal with the uncertainty is focus on what's right in front of you. You cannot focus on the past or what could have happened, either. God willing, you'll live a long, happy life and whatever happens in this case, you'll look back one day and it will seem much more bearable to you. It might not have been your most favorite time in the world, but it will be something contained and definable like that. Not like this ominous, formless cloud hanging over you now. So stay in the 'now' as much as you can and please do not dwell on the past, but look toward your future. Does that make sense?"

"Yep."

With a check of his watch, he set the notepad down.

"Okay, that's it for now. On our next visit I'll have your evaluation complete and we'll know if you're crazy or not."

He smiled, winked, and patted me on the back.

"Let's go see how your mother's doing."

Out in the waiting room, he explained things to my mother.

"I need for both you and your husband to come in and meet with me next time. Do you think that would be possible?"

"Sure. I guess. My husband will have to take some time off from work, but..."

"Well, you work out something that fits your own schedules and call back to make an appointment with my secretary whenever it's good for you, okay?"

"Sure. You ready to go get out of here, Sugarbear?"

"Definitely."

Dr. Delano smiled.

"I'll duly note that nickname in your file."

He shook our hands and returned to his office. We went out into a bitterly cold winter day.

The following Monday, the trial resumed and they finally got around to personal testimony. After lunch they got to Bill Simpson's testimony. It wasn't until Bruno cross-examined the witnesses that the scary truth was brought to light. It was the first time I had heard about Dickie's journey to my house. Dickie had gone to the parties without his own car, plus he was drunk, so he had to beg for a ride over to my place from Bill. In fact, he had begged a half-dozen different people to help him before Bill finally agreed. Dickie had said, if he didn't get a ride, he was going to walk over to my place on his own.

John Walters, Dickie's classmate and neighbor, took the witness stand next and testified to the facts of the party basically as I knew them.

John eventually had to describe Dickie's efforts to get a ride to my place.

"Dickie was going crazy trying to get over to Justin's house. He asked me and about a dozen other people. It wasn't until he threatened to walk there that Bill finally gave in and told him he'd give him a ride. Bill didn't want to do it, though. I could see it by the look on his face. He said 'okay' but it was like he couldn't believe he had agreed to do it. Dickie was acting like such a maniac." I sat there astonished at how much Bruno had uncovered with the DA's witnesses. I asked myself why the DA had called these two guys to testify. Their story seemed to benefit my side of the case more than the DA's.

It was getting late in the day when John Walters climbed down from the stand so Judge Murkowski recessed the trial until the following morning. State Trooper Carl Albert was scheduled to take the stand. It was expected that his testimony would take a very long time.

The next day in court was like pulling teeth. The DA spent hours establishing Officer Albert's background and credentials. Then they went over every little detail of what Officer Albert had been doing the morning of the shooting and what the police had found at the crime scene when they arrived. The day droned on. When Judge Murkowski looked at the clock toward the end of the day and banged his gavel, they still had yet to deal with the actual corpse. Before we recessed for the weekend, it was agreed finally that we would resume things the following Thursday.

With my parents' blessing and the use of their car, I raced over to Maria's place the minute we got back home. Nick and Ellen had ordered pizza and we all sat around and watched a funny movie? We laughed and stuffed ourselves with pizza and I was able to forget about the trial for a little while.

Later on, we cleaned up the kitchen. Nick said goodnight and went upstairs. Ellen turned down the lights.

"What time do you have to be home, Justin?"

"Ten o' clock."

"Okay."

She came over to give me a hug like a mother.

"Make sure you get home on time," she said. "Don't make your mother worry."

"I won't, and thanks for the pizza and everything."

She smiled and hugged me again before heading upstairs. As soon as she was gone, Maria kissed me.

"Let's go talk in my room," she said and led me off by the hand.

The moon was over the lake as we lay on Maria's bed. I heard the furnace kick in. It was chilly outside and you could hear the wind blowing fiercely.

"Are you doing okay with the trial?" Maria asked.

"I guess so. Bruno's sure the judge's verdict will be not guilty."

Maria played with my hair.

"Are you worried at all?"

"Yeah. Of course. All the time. Do you know what freaked me out, though?"

"What's that, babe?"

"John Walters got up on the stand yesterday and testified that Dickie was like a friggin' maniac trying to get over to my house so he could have his way with me. I can't believe Bill brought him. None of this would have happened if no one gave him a ride to my house."

"Yeah, but you know what, Justin? If you keep living in the land of what-could-have-been you're gonna go crazy."

"You're right."

"Okay," she said. "Think about this."

She began to kiss my face and neck and then my chest and once again, Maria found a way to take my mind to a much happier place.

Fourteen

Things were relatively normal the following week at school. That Tuesday, my parents and I made what I hoped would be our final trek down to Dr. Delano's office. After waiting for several minutes in his office. He came out to greet us.

"Mrs. Bailey. Justin."

He shook our hands.

"And a pleasure to meet you, Mr. Bailey. As I've told your wife, you have a real fine young man here."

I didn't like being talked about in the third person, as if I wasn't there, but Dr. Delano's kind words took a bit of the sting out.

"So," he said to me. "You get to sit out in the waiting room and read magazines this time."

"Mr. and Mrs. Bailey, I need to talk with you alone for a bit. Then we'll have Justin come in with us."

He patted me on the back.

"Is that all right, Justin?"

"Sure."

They disappeared into the office. I started thumbing through magazines. Fifteen minutes went by before the door opened again.

"Why don't you come in now, Justin," Dr. Delano said.

I sat with my parents on the couch. Dr. Delano pulled up a chair opposite us.

"At the start of this process, I joked with Justin about finding out whether he was crazy or not. I could joke with him because I knew the minute we spoke that there's nothing crazy about your son. Of course, I'll be submitting my findings reflecting the same to the court."

Dr. Delano looked at me.

"You've been through a lot, young man. A lot more than most kids your age will ever go through and you're handling it quite well. Your mom and dad have told me that you're a great son, but I also knew that with everything we've been through together over the past several weeks."

Dr. Delano smiled at my parents and looked back at me.

"Justin, your parents expressed that they're very concerned about how you're handling this whole ordeal. They're afraid that you're keeping things bottled up inside. Now, as I told them, that is a perfectly average response, but not the healthiest approach to life, so maybe you can make a bigger effort to communicate your thoughts and feelings to them. Can you do that?"

"Yeah sure," I said.

"Good. Well, that's just about it. You're free to go."

He stood up and I got up to give him a hug. Mom and Dad shook his hand.

"Thank you," my father said.

"It's been my pleasure."

Dr. Delano turned to me.

"I'm hoping for the best for you, but remember what I said. Stay focused on the moment right in front of you and please don't dwell on the past."

"Yeah, well, I'm focused on having a brand new car right now."

Dr. Delano laughed.

"Well, that's a little ways into the future, but hopefully not too far."

There were more goodbyes and I got another kind pat on the back as we left.

Later on that week, Officer Albert was back on the stand. The DA and then Bruno questioned Officer Albert about the nature of the gun and the wounds and the angle of the bullets. The DA spent most of that day trying to establish that there were no signs of a physical struggle between Dickie and me. Officer Albert stated that the bullets had been fired from close range. Bruno spent more time pointing out my wounds and cross-examining Officer Albert.

I was so relieved to get out of there on that afternoon, but I was really down and didn't contact any of my friends nor Maria that night. I was still moping around the following day. The gruesome details of that awful encounter had come flooding back with Trooper Albert's testimony and would not leave me alone.

My father came up to my room on Saturday afternoon.

"Justin, I think you need something to help take your mind off this trial."

"Yeah, I suppose," I said.

"No, I'm serious. I talked with your brother Jacob's old boss, Maggie, out at the country club and she's willing to put you on as a banquet waiter a few nights a week. As you probably remember, both of your brothers worked there, so you've got a leg up in terms of reputation, plus it's out in Springfield. There's less of a chance of anyone recognizing you out there."

"Yeah, I guess that's true."

"I think you get to wear a tuxedo. Well, everything but the jacket and you'll probably make some nice tips, too."

He patted me on the shoulder with a smile.

"What do you say? I think it'll help to keep your mind off things."

"Sure, okay. I'm willing to try anything, but what about getting to and from work?"

"We'll figure something out. Either you can take the car or one of us will drive you out there."

"Sure," I said again.

"Good, so why don't we drive out and have a look tomorrow. I'll introduce you to Maggie and I'm sure she'll arrange something that works with your school and the court schedule.

"Don't worry," he added. "She's a very nice lady. She also knows all about what's happened. Not a word will be said."

The next day after church we drove out there and pulled into the golf course parking lot about thirty minutes later. Like my father had said, the country club was a classy place. The clapboard clubhouse was painted white and had a colonial feel to it. The banquet hall overlooked the entire golf course and had a picturesque view down the valley. The place put on all kinds of activities -- member events, golf tournaments, award ceremonies, weddings, proms, and family reunions.

I was filled with apprehension going inside, but Maggie put me at ease at once. We sat and talked in her office for some time but my problems never came up.

"So, what do you think, Justin? Would you like to work here?"

"Sure," I said.

"Well, great," Maggie said, and had a look at her schedule.

"How about if I set you up for two nights this week, just to get you comfortable and we'll go from there."

I looked at my father. He nodded.

"Sure," I said.

"Great," Maggie said. "How about tomorrow night? We'll get you indoctrinated and then I'll have you come in again on Friday night."

Again I looked at my father and again he nodded.

After a bit more chit-chatting, Maggie stood up and held out her hand.

"Welcome aboard, Justin," she said. "And if there's anything I can do to help, please don't hesitate to ask."

Maggie walked us outside.

"By the way, Justin, you're going to love our chef, Jason. He was a big fan of both your brothers."

She shook my father's hand.

"Good to see you, James. We'll take good care of Justin here."

She squeezed me with one arm before heading back into the country club.

"Oh and by the way, we'll provide you with shirt, vest and bowtie. All you'll need is the black dress pants and some nice black shoes. Okay?"

"Sure, thanks," I said.

I started to work the next evening and quickly realized that Dad was right. Everyone from my supervisor to the chef to the other waiters and waitresses made me feel right at home and the job immediately took my mind off the troubles in my life.

On the down side, I was reminded that very night of how my name had traveled far. Several times as I went about my server duties, I became aware of people staring at me. I heard the whispers and realized I could not hope to escape my past by driving to another town.

This point was especially driven home that following Friday when a couple of folks came in for dinner that I thought I remembered seeing at the Hellerman tailgate parties prior to football games.

I worked that entire shift looking over my shoulder. What if his friends recognized me? What if Roy came in to join them? All night long, I was darting glances at the entrance. The same drama kept playing out in my head as I worked. Roy shows up, sees me and starts a scene. I could just picture all the guests stopping with their forks in midair. I had become totally paranoid but could not control myself. I began to question the wisdom of taking this job. The impulse was to hand in my server uniform and head for the hills but nothing came of my fears. Roy never showed up and his friends left without saying a word.

One night a few weeks after I had started, I stopped to buy a soda at a convenience store on the way home. I was minding my own business as usual, but the man in front of me at the checkout stand kept looking back. I thought, oh boy, here we go. I kept my head down and tried to ignore him.

After he had paid for his stuff, he stopped in front of me.

"Hey, aren't you that Justin Bailey I've been seeing in the news lately."

The checker stared. My heart was racing.

"Yeah," I said nervously.

The man looked over his shoulder at the checker and back at me.

"Well, look, I don't mean to embarrass you, Justin, but I just wanted to let you know that my family and I have been following the news and we feel really badly about what you're going through."

He reached out to shake my hand and I accepted.

"I know it must be rough right now with the trial and everything but I wanted to wish you the best of luck."

"Thank you, sir."

He slapped me on the shoulder.

"Well, take care, Justin, and good luck."

"Thank you again."

I fumbled to pay for my soda and walked to my car, almost tearful over his show of support, but tired of my notoriety. None of this would have happened if not for my shooting Dickie.

The following week Dr. Delano came to testify in court. As an expert witness for the trial, he was obligated to play a neutral role but I felt that his sentiments were in my favor. In his opinion I was a sane, well-adjusted young man, and in fact, everything suggested I had acted in self-defense and it couldn't be more clear than that.

Dr. Delano made eye contact with me several times during his testimony and again as he was leaving the courtroom. There was no smile or overt show of support, but I felt his warmth coming through his professional demeanor.

We had several more sessions in court with the DA dragging up a number of students who had been at the parties and expert witnesses who could corroborate various facts. Finally, after weeks of proceedings, the DA rested his case and it was time for the defense.

Bruno brought in several experts and character witnesses of his own to testify. My doctor testified to the physical damage that Dickie caused by beating me.

"If the beating continued, it is possible that Justin would have been left with permanent brain damage," he claimed, just as he had in his office many months ago.

Bruno also called a number of folks from the community to the stand, people who had either witnessed Dickie's drunken activities or had seen him being violent or both. All of their testimonies served to paint a less-than-pretty picture of Dickie's behavior. Then Bruno called on my parents and some friends to testify as to my character and nonviolent nature. In the meantime, Bruno had discussed with my parents the idea of calling me to the witness stand. It was a calculated risk, he admitted. A man does not have to testify against himself, but once he does, anything he says can be used by the district attorney under cross-examination. Still Bruno felt sure it was for the best.

"Ultimately it's up to you, Justin," Bruno said with my parents present. "I feel we need to convey the depth of your fears and anguish throughout the entire event and only you can do that. What do you think?"

I looked at my parents. They nodded.

"Okay, I guess," I said.

The day before I was to take the stand, Bruno ran me through a mock interrogation.

"Each time I ask you a question, you answer that and nothing more. Do you understand?"

"Yes, I understand."

"Now remember, under cross-examination, the DA will be badgering you from a thousand different angles but just do the same thing. Answer his question briefly, directly and nothing more. If the DA gets out of line at all, I'll jump right in. Okay?"

"Okay," I said.

"You'll do fine, Justin," he said.

When it was my turn to testify in court, Bruno looked over and gestured as a way of asking if I was ready. I nodded. He stood up.

"Judge, for my next witness I'd like to ask Justin Bailey to take the stand."

I stood and walked to the front, appearing calm on the outside but riddled with fear and anxiety on the inside. A dozen sets of eyes were upon me. The whole trial might hinge upon my testimony. What if I screwed up?

Bruno asked every question I could have imagined about the events of graduation night - Dickie's behavior at the parties, his following me and taunting me. Then he covered the episode at the house – my fear, Dickie's attacks, my reactions. And yet, his questions were a cakewalk compared to what I was about to face. He had been right. The DA came at me from every conceivable direction. I was petrified and had trouble remaining composed through the relentless questions:

What kind of classes did I take? Did I plan to attend college? Had I ever been expelled from school? Did I have a good relationship with my family?

He tossed some softballs among the most accusatory questions, appearing to try to throw me off. I tried to maintain eye contact with him as he asked each question and gave him the brief, direct answers, just as Bruno had instructed me to do.

Later the DA quizzed me for several minutes about the parties and when I had seen Dickie and what kind of interchanges we had shared over the course of the evening.

"As you were walking around outside, what was the thing that really aggravated Dickie Hellerman."

"Well, he was just looking for a reason to get in a fight. What agitated him was calling him a drunken bum."

"Well, you gave him that reason, then, didn't you?"

"I guess."

And on and on until we were covering the events at my house. His questioning made me feel awful.

Several times the DA suggested that I wasn't scared of Dickie even though he had been beating the crap out of me and that I was goaded into shooting when there were other options open to me like running away. It felt to me like anyone could be the Monday morning quarterback.

"And did the thought to run away and hide somewhere ever occur to you?"

"No. It was my house. The thought of running away never occurred to me."

"Did you consider simply going inside and locking him out?"

"No. I guess I had seen how crazy he was that night and figured he'd just break a window or something."

"Of course either of those actions would have been an option, right?"

"I was very afraid. I just didn't run options through my mind. I just did it. He was coming at me, he was getting angry again."

"But he didn't throw a punch, did he?"

"No."

"He didn't throw a punch, yet you shot him the first time?"

"He was coming after me and I shot the gun."

"And he stopped?"

"Yes."

"You didn't try to run when he stopped, did you?"

"Again, I didn't think. I just reacted. He just stopped for a second and came again."

"He stopped but you didn't try to retreat into the house and close the door?"

"I didn't think. I just reacted. I was terrified. He had already beat me senseless."

When the DA was done, Bruno stood up.

"Re-direct, Your Honor."

"Request granted."

Time passed quickly while Bruno undid many of the misconceptions the DA had tried to create.

At that point, the trial was over except for the verdict. After my testimony that day, Bruno met us outside the courtroom.

"I'm sure the judge is going to exonerate you."

He seemed supremely confident. I went home that night comforted by his words.

On the day of the verdict, I stood as requested.

The judge spoke about having a son just like Dickie who was now a productive member of society. The judge acknowledged his own belief that I had acted in self-defense, but by introducing a gun into the dispute, I had acted recklessly and had forever deprived Dickie of the chance to redeem himself.

The whole time I stood there, my heart was pounding in my chest. My mother and father stood on either side of me, each holding one of my hands. We had been so confident of a "not guilty" verdict, but this was not sounding like a judgment of leniency.

"Therefore," the judge concluded. "On the charge of voluntary manslaughter I find the defendant not guilty. On the charge of involuntary manslaughter, I find the defendant guilty."

And just like that it was done. My mom gasped and held me. All of us stood there in shock. My head was spinning with what his simple statements indicated. I was headed to prison. I felt as if my stomach was going to come up.

The judge read my sentence next. I was to be locked up until at least my 21st birthday. I could continue with my senior year of classes, but as soon as I had received the necessary credits to graduate, I was to begin serving my sentence at the juvenile state prison. Beyond attending my senior classes, I was forbidden from participating in any senior activities. That meant no prom, no senior class trip, no graduation.

Bruno led us from the main courtroom to another room nearby, where he explained what to expect next and exactly what the verdict meant. My parents kept asking him how this could happen. Bruno had been so sure. It made no sense. Even the judge had admitted I was justified in shooting Dickie, so why the guilty verdict? I sat there in silence. I imagined myself in prison being bullied by a bunch of gang bangers.

I vaguely heard Bruno explaining the difference between voluntary and involuntary manslaughter charges.

"It's like you told Dickie to put an apple on his head, only when you tried to shoot the apple, you accidentally shot him instead. The intent to kill was not there."

Bruno seemed very impressed with this subtlety of law and indignant about my going to jail, but I was going anyway.

As part of my sentence, I had also been placed on probation and given a curfew. I had to be home every night by 9 o'clock at the latest.

As much as the Hellermans had wanted the death penalty, they still gloated over my misfortune. Friend after friend stopped me at school. "Dude, this is so unfair." I walked around in a daze.

A few weeks later, I was at Maria's house one night and lost track of time. I looked at my watch and saw that it was already 8:50 pm. The drive home took more than fifteen minutes. I was going to blow my probation.

"Oh man, I'm late," I said, grabbing the keys to the car and giving Maria a quick goodbye kiss before I dashed out the door.

As I rocketed along on the narrow, back country roads, I nervously lit up a cigarette. When my tires screeched around a particularly sharp turn, I slowed down a bit but then sped up again. I was flying up and down the hills on my way home.

A few miles short of our driveway, I started to put out my cigarette in the ashtray and watched it fly off onto the floorboard. In a panic, I bent down to retrieve it. Doing sixty, I took my eyes off the narrow road.

The last thing I remembered was the car jouncing up and down on rough terrain and a tree flying at me, followed by a horrific crashing sound and my face hurtling forward into the front windshield. Then all was silent.

I came to with the car on its side and the horn blaring hours later. My face was bloody. It was completely dark on that empty road.

I got out, thinking I might be able to turn the car back over, but in planting my left foot on the ground, I doubled over in pain. My ankle had been twisted and broken. I almost fainted at the sight of it.

I waited for some time for a car to go by before I began to hobble and hop down the road in search of help. I had limped along in this manner for over a mile when I saw a house in the distance and went up to ring the doorbell. No one answered so I knocked hard on the door. A woman finally answered it. Weak from the trauma and loss of blood, I fell into her arms. She screamed to her husband to help. I passed out and did not awaken again until I was in a hospital bed. My mom and dad were at my bedside. My mom hugged and kissed me profusely. My father patted me on the arm.

"What the hell happened?" he asked.

"Honey!" Mom said to him "Your son just had a terrible accident."

"I know. That's why I'm trying to figure out what went on out there."

"Just stop it, all right?"

She turned to me.

"We're just so glad you weren't killed, honey."

She hugged me again.

The next day they wheeled me into surgery and repaired my ankle with a plate and four screws. I awakened with a cast on my foot.

My friends Donnie, Ethan and Ted came by to see me. Maria was there night and day, as were my parents. I finally had to explain the cause of the accident. My father wasn't very happy to hear it.

A couple of days later, I was released from the hospital. The doctor told me to rest for a week before returning to school. My mom stayed around taking care of me. On the third day, she asked if I would join her on some errands.

"No," I said, without explaining myself. I was so depressed about life in general, that I really didn't even want to move.

"Come on, Sugarbear," she insisted. "I don't want you moping around the house all by yourself."

"I'm not moping."

She gave me a look.

"All right, I'll go."

Ten minutes later, we were heading off in her new car. Just like the last car, it was an economy number, but at least it had power windows. My mom showed me the features and made small talk.

"Where are we going?" I asked her.

"We're going to the bank, the grocery store and to the insurance company."

I sat there half asleep in the passenger seat while Mom drove from location to location. She fumbled with the radio dial and found something she thought I would like.

"There you go, Sugarbear. KRX FM. Isn't that your favorite?"

I offered her a feeble smile. She winked and patted me on my good leg.

While she was in the bank, I dozed off. I awakened again when she came back out and opened the door.

"Next stop the insurance company and then the supermarket. Maybe we can get that chocolate ice cream you really like."

"Now that's what I'm talking about, Mom."

My crappy mood improved a bit.

At the insurance company, my mom left me in the parked car again.

"I'll be right out. I just have to make a quick payment."

She was out in a couple of minutes and we headed across town to Gary's Market. It was a small grocery store a few miles from our house.

"Aren't you coming in?" she asked when we got there.

"I don't know."

"Come on. It won't take long."

"All right," I said reluctantly.

Inside the market, she made her way very slowly down the aisles so I could keep up with my crutches. I watched her load up on laundry detergent, spaghetti sauce, lettuce, tomatoes and finally my chocolate ice cream.

As we drove along, she turned the opposite way of home.

"What's going on?"

"I need to make one more stop, hunny."

I groaned and slumped back down in the seat. The radio was playing *Huey Lewis* in the background. My mom headed out through the back roads for fifteen minutes or so. When she turned into Carlyle's junkyard, my attention perked up.

"What are we doing here?"

"Look over there," she pointed. "I wanted you to see something."

She was pointing through the chain link fence.

"Can you see it?"

I searched among the many wrecks until I saw the car I had wrecked. Mom helped me out with my crutches and we both went over to the fence.

"Holy crap!" I exclaimed.

I had not seen the car since the night of the crash and even then my memory of it was foggy at best. In the light of day, the car was barely recognizable having been wrapped around a tree. I looked over to my mom. She had tears pouring down her cheeks.

"It's a wonder that you're alive, you know that?"

She reached over and pulled me close.

"I love you so much, honey. God must have plans for you because he kept you here on earth with me."

I was fighting back tears, too.

"I'm so sorry, Mom. I never meant to cause you so much trouble."

"Oh, don't you say that, Sugarbear. I'm just so glad you're still alive."

She held me to her breast.

"Hey, we'd better get that chocolate ice cream home before it all melts."

She helped me back into the car with my crutches and we made a slow u-turn away from the junkyard. There was just enough time to have a final look at the wrecked car. The question struck me again, as it had in the days after Dickie's death. Why me? Why was I alive? I stared over my shoulder at the junkyard until my mom had turned around the next bend. Wow, I thought and shook my head. By the looks of the car, it did seem like a miracle that I had survived the crash.

The following Monday, I was cleared to go back to school. I had grown very antsy and was glad to get out of the house, but hobbled out toward the building with new cause for apprehension. I was trying to lay low but one more time I was the center of attention.

My classmates crowded around me first thing. As was usual in our small town, everyone already knew the whole story of my accident.

"Hey," one girl said when I finished recounting the accident. "I'll bet you're excited."

"About what?"

"The yearbooks are coming out today, dummy."

"Oh wow. I'd completely forgotten."

She gave me a pat on the shoulder and went on her way. I thought back to the previous year, when I had ditched class to sneak into everyone else's homeroom and become part of their photos. Before the accident, I had been waiting with great anticipation. I expected to see my face plastered throughout the pages.

The yearbooks weren't released until after our final class. Students had been talking about it with great excitement all day and when the final bell rang, we all hurried out to gather in groups around the hallways and gymnasium. With great anticipation, I opened my yearbook and felt slapped in the face. The first page was a gigantic photo homage to Dickie Hellerman. "In Fond Memory" it read. I shut the yearbook. There were stares from my fellow students. The nightmare had returned. A boy was dead and I was responsible for killing him. There were no fond memories for me.

As soon as it was convenient, I slipped out of school and headed home that afternoon, haunted by the tribute to Dickie the entire way. Out by my father's firing range, I started a fire in our burn barrel and when the flames were high enough, ripped out Dickie's photo page first and threw it into the fire. I tore out huge handfuls until every page of the yearbook had been burned. Hindered by the crutches, it was a quite a spectacle. By the end I was cursing everything in sight. With bitter irony, I realized the big photo of Dickie had been taken the night I played host to *The Coneheads' Family Feud*. I had been on top of the world myself with all the attention. Life was good then for me. Now he was dead and the joy of life had been ripped from my life. I stared in silence with tears streaming down my face as the pages burned and fluttered away as ashes.

Defending My Life

Fifteen

All through those final months of my senior year, I had secretly fretted over what lay in store for me. Someway, somehow, the day would come for me to surrender and start serving my sentence in a juvenile detention facility. The judge had ruled I was to be incarcerated as soon as I had sufficient credits to graduate, but no one had explained to me exactly how this was to be implemented. Nothing more specific had been said. I was kept in the dark.

In the absence of specific information, my mind devised all sorts of fanciful endings. Perhaps they had forgotten about me. Perhaps I would be forgiven. My mind indulged itself with any number of such wishful daydreams, only to snap back to the stressful reality. The day was coming. I didn't know when, only that my graduation would inevitably be followed with my being led off to prison. I lived with this grim realization every day.

To make matters worse, all my classmates went off to Washington D.C. for the senior graduation trip and, per Judge Murkowski's instructions, I was not allowed to go. I sat around feeling sorry for myself that entire weekend, left to imagine what a great time everyone was having.

When my friends got back, I pretended not to give a crap as they told me what a great time they had had. Having been denied the right to go really hit me hard. As everyone related their stories, I secretly hated them for making it sound like so much fun.

The following day, Donnie and I were on our way to school when he pulled into the convenience store.

"I need some cigarettes, dude? You want anything from inside?"

"I'm going in to get a candy bar and a soda."

I followed him into the store on my crutches. A minute later, Donnie was up front at the counter paying for his cigarettes. I was still back in the snack aisle making up my mind.

"Hey, Justin," he called to me. "I'll see you out in the car."

"Okay, I'll be there in a minute."

I ditched the candy bar, went for some chips and was headed for the front counter when I heard someone say "hey, shooter" from behind me.

I turned to find Roy Hellerman Jr. heading down the aisle in my direction. He had the same hate-filled look on his face that I had seen the day he watched me wrestle, in fact the same look I had seen on the faces of all the Hellermans.

"You're going down, shooter!" Roy said.

I hurried up to the counter. The clerk was in back somewhere. I turned to face Roy. My thought was to drop my stuff and hurry off with my crutches but Roy had me cornered.

"You're going down, shooter," he said again.

"Can I help you?" the clerk said over my shoulder.

"Yeah, just this," I said and pointed at my stuff on the counter.

With a glance behind me, I saw Roy backing his way out of the door. He pointed a finger at me and left.

"Is everything all right?" the clerk asked.

"Yeah, yeah," I said, and fumbled to pay him.

"I can call the cops if you want," the clerk said as he handed me my change.

"No, it's all right," I said. "He's leaving."

I took my snacks and went to look out the door. Roy had gotten into his car and was driving slowly towards the street, his focus still on me.

As soon as Roy's car hit the street, I dashed out to Donnie's car. Donnie was nodding out with his eyes closed and the music on full blast. I pulled the car door open, hopped in and slammed it shut.

"Damn, dude," Donnie said. "Take it easy on the door. You know this Subaru is already falling apart."

"I just saw Roy Jr. in the store."

"What!?"

Donnie turned the music down and looked all around.

"Out there."

I pointed.

"That's him pulling away. He came after me in the store but left when the clerk saw him. He said, 'You're going down, shooter.'"

"What the hell!"

"Yeah, just get the heck out of here, man, before he comes back."

Donnie turned around in the parking lot and peeled out down the road. My heart was racing on the way to school. I thought of being locked up on one side of me and the threat of death on the other. I was beginning to view being locked up as the lesser of two evils. At least when I got out of prison I'd still be alive. I wasn't so sure about surviving Roy Jr. I began to think that the torment would never end. The thought of perpetually being bullied by the Hellerman family was very depressing and frustrating.

I considered calling the cops but realized it was rather

pointless. After all the things I had already been through, I didn't want any more problems. I just wished I could move away or something.

Toward the end of May, I turned in the last of my term papers. My classes were now all completed. Graduation was a formality. The guillotine hung over my head, though no one had told me yet when it was supposed to drop. There had been no discussion with me about the date for the start of my prison sentence.

That week, my brother Noah came home on leave from his tour in the Air Force. He had been stationed in Holland and assigned to the military police. I was overjoyed by his presence. Noah was a few years older than I, but the two of us had been the best of friends growing up.

The day he arrived, we had a family dinner together. The next day, Noah and I arranged to go out and have pizza by ourselves.

"Lakeview Deli fine with you?" he asked as he pulled out onto the road.

"Yeah, sure, they have great pizza," I said.

Once we had ordered and settled in with our drinks, Noah asked me what had been happening. How was I doing? Did I need to get anything off my chest? Our talk led us back to the night of the shooting.

"This is kind of where it started," I said and pointed out the window. "I mean, Maria and I were walking down that road right around the corner from here when Dickie and his friends came out to harass us. That's when I called him a drunken bum. Who knew calling him a drunken bum was the one thing that would put him over the edge."

"Well, he was a drunken bum," Noah said. "I see it all the time in my work as an MP. They're the nicest people in the world when they're sober, then they take a drink and they turn into monsters."

I nodded in agreement.

"What I'm saying is, maybe Dickie felt that way. Maybe he wanted someone to put him out of his misery. It sure sounded like he had a death wish from the things he said to you that night."

"Dickie threatened to kill himself and his whole family right after Randy's party! I saw the police report."

"See, there you go."

I had been watching our waitress and noticed when she went to make a phone call after bringing us our drinks.

"You know that chick, our waitress?"

Noah turned to look at her and back at me.

"Yeah, that one over there."

"What about her?"

"She's close with the Hellerman family, I think."

"So?"

"So, I saw her make a call after she served us our drinks."

"What, you think she called the Hellermans?"

"Yeah, maybe."

Noah smiled and sipped his soda.

"You're getting a little paranoid, kid."

The pizza came and we dug into our food. A few minutes later the front door opened and Roy Jr. walked in.

"Oh no, not again," I groaned.

Noah looked and immediately started to get up. I grabbed hold of his arm.

"Please don't. I don't need any more drama in my life right now."

"I'm not going to kick his ass, as much as I'd like to. I'm just going to suggest he pick on someone his own size. And tell the manager about his stupid friggin' employee. I can't believe that idiot called him."

Again I pulled on Noah's arm.

"Look, I really appreciate your looking out for me, but it's already hard enough on me living in this town. I don't need another scene."

Noah reluctantly settled back in, but kept glancing over his shoulder at Roy. Roy stood for a half minute over on the far side of the small restaurant and then went back out to lean against his car in the parking lot. We could see him through the big picture window.

"The guy's a friggin' coward," Noah said. "Just like his brother. Always picking on someone smaller than themselves."

I stared down at my pizza, shaking my head. Why is this stuff always happening to me, I thought. I wasn't hungry anymore either.

"Hey," Noah said. "Sorry. Let's just drop it and talk about something else. I'm proud of you, you know? You had every right to defend yourself and you're handling this like a real trooper."

We tried to focus on our food and more pleasant conversation. The discussion turned to days gone by filled with innocence and wonder when we were young, like vacations in Ocean City during the summer. Noah shared stories of his Air Force life and his time in Amsterdam.

When the waitress brought our check, I tried to dissuade Noah from commenting again but he spoke up anyway.

"Yeah, we know you called your buddy out there. You're lucky I don't tell the manager."

She left looking both angry and red-faced.

"Bitch," Noah added under his breath. That was my brother, never afraid to defend what he thought was right.

When we went out to the parking lot, Roy got into his car. Noah drove off very slowly, as if he were inviting Roy to follow us, but Roy only stared as we headed down the road.

Noah flew back to Holland a few days later. Graduation was right around the corner. I spent each day secretly wondering when the end would come.

About two weeks before school let out, my parents came by to pick me in the afternoon, but instead of heading for home, my father turned in the other direction.

"Where are we going?" I asked.

Mom looked over the front seat at me.

"Oh, we've got something to take care of in the city."

We drove in silence for miles. Frequently, I observed my dad looking in the rearview mirror at me. When we came to the juvenile detention center, he turned into the driveway and started up the hill. My heart began to race.

"What's going on?" I asked.

Dad looked at me again in the rearview mirror.

"We just need to take care of some paperwork," he said.

I stared out of the window of the car as we approached the ominous-looking brick building. There were bars on every window. I had noticed this building every time we went to court in the previous months.

I would be thinking to myself, glad I don't live there…

Now my dad was stopping in front of the building.

He got out, my mom did the same. They helped me with my crutches and we headed toward the entry, me humping along beside them.

Inside, two uniformed men greeted us. They led us down several passageways. When we came to a small room, the men left us alone. My folks faced me with pained looks on their faces.

"You have to stay here now, honey," Mom said.

I dropped into a chair and broke down. My mom came over to comfort me. My dad was holding her. The three of us cried together.

"I don't get it," I said, once I had gathered myself. "Who decided it had to be today? When did you find out?"

"We received a certified letter ten days ago," my father explained. "It said you were to surrender today."

"God, why didn't you tell me?" I asked.

"Look, son, I've been a wreck since the day the letter arrived."

He looked at Mom.

"We've both been a mess," she said. "We cried together for hours that day, but after a long discussion and taking time to consider things, we decided it would have only ruined the rest of your school activities if we told you."

I sat there, head in hand, filled with anguish.

"I don't even get to graduate with my friends now."

"Bruno's trying to work out something about that," my mom said.

I continued to sob.

"I'm sorry, I'm sorry, I'm sorry," Mom repeated, holding my head close to her. "Please understand how difficult this was for us."

My mom pulled my head up to look at her.

"We weren't sure if it was the right thing to do, but we were only thinking of you. You got to have nine more regular days without all the anxiety and stress of knowing the exact plans weighing down on you, normal days that you would not have had if we had told you. I hope you can forgive us."

At this point, the two uniformed men returned to the room. My dad looked at his watch and nodded. One of the men opened a door. I saw that it led into the adjoining lockup area. The other uniformed man directed me toward the door. My parents hugged me a final time.

"Don't worry, son. We'll be out here fighting for you every day."

When I resisted, the second man helped to pull me through the door.

"No please, I'm not ready for this!" I begged.

"We love you, honey," Mom said.

I heard both my parents repeating this as the door closed. One of the men pointed down the corridor. I stumbled along between the two guards, tears rolling down my face.

In the intake room, I was instructed to sit down. My crutches were placed out of the way. The enormity of everything settled over me. It seemed impossible that I was here. How did this happen? Just that day I had been hanging out with my friends. I had been making plans to see Maria for the weekend. My mind was swimming with the incredulity of it all. I didn't even get a chance to say goodbye to anyone.

A man helped me over to a table and took my fingerprints. With that done, my crutches were returned and I was led into another room. There was a shower and a small opening into a different room.

"Take off your clothes," one of the guards said.

With that done, he told me to get into the shower.

"I'm not supposed to shower with this cast on."

"All right," he said. "Just wait there."

I stood there, naked and shivering. The guard came back with a black plastic bag. He placed it over the cast and cinched it off with a big rubber band.

"Now, hold your hands up," he said and sprayed me with something pungent.

"What is this?" I asked.

"It's to delouse you."

After he had sprayed my front, he told me to turn around and bend over.

"All right," he said when he was done. "Take a shower. You've got three minutes."

I hobbled around in there with my bum ankle. While I was showering, the man brought out an orange prison outfit. He stood and watched me.

Once I had dried off, he hit my genitals with a powder.

"What's that for?" I asked.

"It's to kill vermin."

Vermin, I thought. What kind of people do they bring into this place, anyway?

After I was all dressed in county orange, the guard led me toward the far door. I heard a buzz of voices on the other side and assumed this was a common area for the inmates. I had visions of one of my father's prison stories. As soon as the guard left me alone, some tough guy would come beat the crap out of me.

The door opened and I was faced with a sea of young men in the same orange jumpsuits. The letters GCDC were imprinted on each jumpsuit. The guard showed me to my cell. The other inmates hooted and called out names as we went by.

The cell was not spacious by any stretch of the imagination - eight feet by twelve feet, with a bed, a metal sink and a metal toilet with no seat. The bed had a thick wool blanket and one pillow. I felt the bed. It seemed to be filled with hay and smelled like it had been in the cell for twenty years. The pillowcase was little more than a plastic tarp. While this was a jail for juvenile offenders, there was little to distinguish it from every image I had ever had of an adult jail. On the plus side, I did not have a roommate.

Needing to blow my nose, I looked around the cell for some toilet paper but found none.

I explained to the guard. He went off and came back with enough toilet paper for one shot.

"I can't have a roll?"

"No. If you need more, you ask us for it," he said sternly.

I wondered what in the world they thought you would do with the excess supply. Hang myself?

Next, the guard led me out to the common area and quickly left. A small crowd of boys approached me.

"Whatcha in for?" someone asked. Young men were pushing in from all sides. I kept my head down and tried to walk away, praying they'd leave me alone.

"Come on, whatcha in for?" someone else asked again.

Everywhere I turned, I was dive-bombed and badgered with the same question by the inmates. What was the nature of my crime? Jostled on all sides, I finally mumbled to one of them that I wasn't proud of what I had done and didn't want to talk about it. As I should have expected, this only ramped up their curiosity.

Frustrated, I finally shouted out, "I freakin' killed somebody, all right?"

A total silence fell over the area. Then the buzz of voices rose to a new crescendo.

"Wow, dude, that's hardcore," one kid said.

"Yeah, most of us are in here for stealing car stereos or selling drugs."

There was laughter.

"Or 'cuz nobody wanted us so we smashed some windows just to get off the streets and have a roof over our heads."

"Come on, dude," the first kid said. "You've got to lay it out, man."

Seeing no way around it, I started to explain my story. As new kids came around, I sometimes had to relate the grisly parts again. The afternoon rushed away while I told my tale and answered all their questions.

When the inquisition finally ended, I wandered off to be alone. There was a smaller recreation room off to one side of the common area and I went in there to watch TV. The news was playing. The television was up by the ceiling. Someone told me the guards kept the remote. That fact served to drive my new lack of freedom home to me even more. Something as minor as changing the channel and you had to get a guard to do it.

A short time later the dinner bell rang and I followed the rush of inmates to a line outside the cafeteria. As we filed in, I followed the lead of everyone else and picked up a tray. Both crutches went under one arm. I hopped along on my good leg. When it was my turn, some food was slopped onto the tray. I tried to get back to a table without dumping the whole thing onto the floor.

I sat and ate in silence. The chaos around me was torment to my soul. I was going nuts after being imprisoned for only a few hours and I had three years minimum in front of me. Bruno had filed an appeal, which offered some potential hope, but there were no guarantees he would succeed. Meanwhile, the days, weeks and months of my life would slip away, but ever so slowly.

Later in the evening another bell rang. It was time to return to our cells. When the door slammed shut and the lights went out, I broke down and cried. The awful smelling straw-filled bed, the steel bars, the loneliness, all combined to depress me and make me think my life was doomed. When a guard came by on his rounds, I asked him for more toilet paper and eventually cried myself to sleep.

In the morning, I woke up to the sound of my cell door sliding open. A guard was screaming at everyone to get up. I had slept in my orange jumpsuit and simply had to climb out of bed. Lines were forming for the morning chow. I followed along on my crutches. The same awkward routine from the previous meal ensued.

Shortly after breakfast, a guard called my name and I was ushered back into the processing room. I thought perhaps my parents had come to see me, or better yet, Bruno had been successful with the appeal. Instead, the guard told me to strip. He took my jumpsuit. I got back my street clothes. The Greenville County Detention Center had only been a holding spot for the night. I was headed to a more permanent facility. My heart sank at the sound of it. Greenville County Detention Center had been a dark, dingy and ominous place. I had no expectation of things getting better.

Once I had been out-processed, two plainclothes cops led me outside to a Crown Victoria. They took my crutches, handcuffed me and helped me into the back seat. There were bars separating the front seat from the back.

"Where are we going?" I asked the driver as he turned the car around and headed down the hill. Neither he nor the other man bothered to look over the seat or acknowledge my question.

Exhausted from the trauma of the previous day, I leaned back and fell asleep. Every once in a while I woke up from the discomfort of having my hands cuffed behind my back.

Several hours later, I woke up for good and looked out through the window. I had no idea where I was. The man riding shotgun looked back at me and forward again without saying a word. It suddenly dawned on me. To them, I was a killer, a criminal. I was having a real hard time seeing myself in that way.

We were driving through country much like the area around my hometown, winding back roads, fields and farmland. It broke my heart to see it. I wanted so much to get out and run free.

I saw a sign for some historic landmark. Soon after that sign, the driver turned into the entrance of a parking lot. A large brick building was at the far end of the parking lot. The building had almost a cathedral-like quality to it. The wide lawns around the building were surrounded by trees and open country. I saw a sign that read Saint Jude's Hall for Boys.

The driver parked the car, then the other guard helped me out, removed the hand cuffs and handed me my crutches again. We entered the facility through an arched opening beneath one of the spires. My escorts handed my files to an elderly lady and left.

"How did you break your leg?" she asked, in a way that suggested she actually cared.

While I explained the accident, a tall, lean black man came in. I had never been face to face with a black person before in my life. There were none in our school or anywhere in our town, at least none that I had met. This man had a kind face. His hair color had turned salt and pepper.

Once the elderly lady had finished with processing me, I was turned over to the black gentleman.

"My name's Mike," he said.

"I'm Justin."

He shook my hand and led me out to a hallway. I hobbled along slowly beside him with my crutches.

All along the hallway there was a dark, maple wainscoting on the walls, with columns every twenty feet or so. This building definitely did not start out as a detention center. It had that musty scent that most old buildings have.

"Intake is all the way up on the top floor," Mike said with a bemused look of concern. "You sure you're going to make it all right?"

"Pretty sure. My bedroom is upstairs at home so I've been getting a lot of practice."

Mike shook his head.

"You don't much look like the kind who belongs in here, young man."

"Can I leave then?"

He laughed.

"Well, I think some folks would be greatly upset if I let you go."

"I probably wouldn't get very far, anyway."

"No, I suspect a young man trucking down the highway on crutches would be a dead giveaway."

We came to a maple staircase and started up together. I held my crutches in one hand and the handrail with the other. Mike walked along beside me as I hopped up step by step.

"If it's any consolation," he said. "This is about as good as it gets when it comes to doing time. Nothing like that detention center where you were. I've been there a few times and man, what that place will do to some of these young men!"

"Yeah," I said. "This place is definitely an upgrade."

The Greenville County Detention Center had made me feel like a hardcore criminal. Mistrust surrounded you. At least here Mike and the old lady had made me feel like I was a kid again.

We came to the third landing and I stopped to catch my breath.

"How much farther?"

"This is the fourth floor. Intake is on the seventh floor."

"Oh, man. Don't they have an elevator?"

"We can take you back to Greenville if you like."

"No thank you," I said and started hopping up the next flight of stairs.

Coming to the seventh floor, we walked into a madhouse. I had never been to the inner city but knew that's where they had found these kids. The guys ranged from seven- or eight-year-olds to kids my own age. Suddenly, I was one of the elders.

"Take care, son," Mike said, with a pat on the shoulder.

I watched him head back down the stairs, saddened to see him go. The man had emanated kindness and wisdom and I had little hope of finding those traits anywhere else inside a juvenile prison. Confirming my suspicions, the new guard led me off to my cubicle without saying a word.

I was at least encouraged by the cubicle itself. It had carpet and a desk. The bed was modestly comfortable. The pillowcase was softer than a plastic tarp. Plus there were no bars on the windows.

The guard showed me the rest of the facilities, which included a public restroom with urinals, toilets and showers. A short lecture on the do's and don'ts followed. Then I was released into the general lockup.

Straight off, a crowd of kids came over and hit me with questions. It was the same stuff I had been asked up at Greenville. "What are you in for? Tell us all about it." From the previous experience I had learned to condense things down considerably. When they heard I had killed someone, word spread quickly throughout intake. When I finally took a stroll through the facility, everyone I met had already heard the story.

That night after dinner and recreation time, we were taken down to the yard to walk. I think the idea was to wear us down a bit before hitting the hay. In my case they could have skipped the yard time. Hopping up seven flights of stairs alone had worn me out.

I crawled into bed half an hour later, hating where I was, but as all people will do under the same circumstances, I busied myself with conjuring up thoughts of better days.

Sixteen

The next day, my fellow inmates filled me in on the nuts and bolts of how Saint Jude's worked. The residents were broken down into separate age groups with each of those groups containing roughly 10 to 20 inmates. These inner city kids, ranging in ages from 8 to 18, had been locked up for everything from selling drugs to stealing cars. It was minimum security, which explained the lack of fences and bars on the windows. As it turned out, I was the only kid in there from a rural area.

Everybody was considered "intake" when they first came in and outfitted with a red shirt to signify this fact. Eventually we would all be relocated to a different part of the lock up with kids our own age. Thank God. I couldn't wait to get out of that madhouse. Ridiculous little fights were breaking out everywhere I looked.

Seven days later, I was transferred to a sub-unit called Beta House. When they called my name, I was taken back to the processing area and handed a couple of yellow shirts. Each age group had its own designated color. That way the guards could tell at a glance where you belonged. I also received a care package from my parents. It contained candy and gum and two letters. One was from my parents, the other from Maria.

While I waited with my shirts and care package, Mike came in.

I was glad to see him again. There was something so comforting about his kind smile and demeanor.

"Justin, pack up your things!" the guard yelled. 'You're going with Mike!"

Pleased with that news, I pulled myself up with my crutches to greet Mike. He gave me a pat on the back and grabbed my bags.

"Beta House is on the 2nd floor," he said as we headed back down.

"Oh, cool. That's a relief to hear."

Mike again went slowly so I could keep up with my crutches.

"So, how's it going for you?" he asked with a kind smile.

"All right. The kids are crazy up there."

"Yeah, you know most of these kids have had to raise themselves."

He looked over at me.

"For the most part."

"Really?"

"Yeah, most of the youngest ones were born to crackhead mothers who never gave their children a second thought. They have nothing else in this world."

Up to that point, I had never considered anyone else's background. I had only been thinking of myself.

"Wow. Are you serious?"

"It is what it is, Justin. They have it better in here than they'd have it on the outside."

Neither of us spoke again until we arrived at the Beta unit. It was break time and all of the other inmates in my new unit were out in the yard.

"Good time to sneak in and set up camp," Mike said. "And believe me, you're lucky. This is a little subdivision of Beta. I think only nine others are in here with you and you all have your own little space."

He showed me to my cubicle inside a large room. Each cubicle was outfitted with a bed, a small closet, a dresser and a desk with a little lamp. There was something especially old and musty about this part of the building, but it was still a million times better than the first lockup.

Mike sat down while I unpacked my few things.

"You miss your folks, Justin?"

I stopped.

"Yeah. And my girlfriend."

"You got yourself a little sweetheart, do you?"

"Yeah."

I told Mike about her. There was a pause. I wasn't sure whether or not to explain her involvement and how it had played into what happened but I did.

"That's real tough," Mike said. "Men have been fighting over women since the world began."

I sat down and looked out the window.

"I wish I could walk out there right now. It's driving me crazy knowing I can't."

"You will someday. In the meantime, take care and be good and maybe you can go out with us to a ballgame this summer."

"A ballgame?"

"We have a contest in here called the "Summer of Fun." You behave yourself like a saint and you can get picked to go on a field trip each month. We already have one planned to a theme park, and like I said, we're going down to see a pro baseball game, too."

"Wow. Really? That sounds too cool. What do you do? Chain everybody together so they won't run away?"

Mike laughed.

"You're forgetting, Justin. You try to run away and it only gets worse."

Mike stood up.

"So, like I said, behave yourself and I'll see to it that you get full consideration."

He patted me gently on the back.

"Well, make yourself at home. I'm headed back to take care of some paperwork. I'm sure I'll see you around here soon."

I had hardly gotten comfortable when the other members of Beta came in from their break. The questions started in.

"So whatcha in for? Who did you kill?"

My story had spread before me but the details were still required and I reluctantly gave them. Retelling the experience became like repeating the same word over and over again. The whole thing started to sound unreal to me. Either way, I had no desire to relive those moments, but having killed someone earned me a lot of cachet in that place. Any other white kid weighing a hundred pounds would have had his ass kicked a dozen times by then. The way fights broke out around there, you had to figure as much.

The fights were always about stupid stuff. The guards came rushing in to break it up. The guilty parties were sent away for a few days. Then they reappeared and the fighting started all over again.

I was referred to as "Shooter" by some of the other inmates. I didn't like it, but it kept me from being bothered, so I kept my mouth shut.

The days quickly turned into a routine. Sometimes things were all right. Sometimes I felt melancholy. Late at night when it was quiet, I would lie in bed thinking about Maria and my life back at home.

I became close with two inner city kids named Stanley and Darnell. Like a lot of kids, they were in for something minor. They were funny as hell and made me laugh a lot. Lying in bed at night I would listen to the two of them talking and joking around.

Darnell was a skinny little dude like me, with a shaved head and a gold chain around his neck. He played basketball with Stan and a real big guy named Jamal. Darnell's bunk was right next to mine. The only thing that separated our cubicles was a short 2 x 4 wall. Late at night he and I would get into lengthy discussions. He was in for petty theft, a lot of petty theft. He seemed like a really decent person at heart who had been trapped into a crappy life. His family lived in the city. They were extremely poor.

One night, we were watching TV after dinner and this white kid named Sean came over to where I was sitting. He was scrawnier than me and wore his hair like Vanilla Ice. I think he believed that the color of our skin unified us, but instead, I got stressed out just being around him. He was always wound up like a top.

"Hey, bro," he said and sat next to me. I moved over.

Stan and Darnell were keeping an eye on things.

"So, what? That's your boy." Stanley said with a laugh. He and his whole crowd were having a good laugh.

"He isn't my boy," I said and moved further away.

"Looks like your boy to me," Stan said, staying on me.

Jamal had the remote and changed to MTV. And like magic, *Vanilla Ice* came on doing "Ice Ice, Baby." Sean jumped up into the middle of the room.

"Yo yo yo, I got crazy skills, yo."

He mimicked the dance routine and sang along. Everybody except me was in stitches. Sean had no idea they were laughing at him, not with him. The guy didn't have enough brains to know the difference.

Stanley and the others were doubled over in laughter.

"That's your boy," Stan said when he could catch his breath. "That's your boy."

Sean was showing off for me now. I buried my head in embarrassment.

That night out in the yard for our bedtime walk, Sean came up and told me how you could get you high by adding toothpaste to a cigarette. Seeing again how really whacked out this clown was, I moved away. Associating with him too closely was clearly not in my best interest.

Lying awake in bed that night, Darnell and I got into talking about our lives as kids. I told him a story about going to a football game in the town where I lived and being amazed at how much better the city kids were than the players in my high school.

"You mean you ain't never seen no black folk before in your life?!"

"Well, I guess not really. Not face to face."

"Man, that's messed up. You hear that, Stan?"

A guard came by and told us to keep it down. We waited until he had disappeared to the other end of the ward.

"I remember my grandmother telling me once when I was a kid that she'd never even think about touching a black person."

Darnell fell out of his bed, laughing. He got up and came after me.

"Here I come, man. I'm gonna touch your ass."

He calmed down a minute later and was suddenly serious.

"You know, Justin, I miss my lady, and my little girl."

"What, you're married and have a kid?"

"No, I ain't married, but yeah, me and my lady got a little girl."

I was shocked to think he was already a father. He was younger than I was. Darnell pulled a picture of a little girl out of his wallet.

"Look at this. How the heck can I be locked up in here?"

I handed the picture back to him. The little girl was so cute, all smiles with pretty pink bows in her hair and filled with hope. What a trip. Darnell always came off as this little prankster. Suddenly he was a serious father.

"Hey," Darnell said before we went to sleep.

"Yeah?" I said.

"You know that ole knucklehead cracker?"

"You mean Sean?"

"Yeah."

"So, what about him?"

"You better watch out. He ain't nothing but trouble. Everybody here steers clear of that cracker."

"Thanks for the tip, but I already know that."

The next day, Darnell and Stanley were back to giving me grief about being brought up around only white people.

"Man, how do you like that?" Stanley said to Darnell. "This cracker ain't got no black folk in his town."

"We're just gonna have to go up there and screw things up for these white folks, Stanley."

Stan looked over at me.

"That is goddamned amazing. No black folk. Hmm, hmm, hmm."

I had never given it much thought until the previous night when I was talking with Darnell, but it was rather amazing how homogenized my hometown had been.

Later on that week, I was sitting in the yard on a sunny afternoon when a guard came over to my bench.

"Justin, you have to come with me. They're asking for you in the warden's office."

The warden, I thought. Oh no. I had never met him up to that point and immediately was worried sick. There could be no reason for him wanting to see me unless it was a lousy one.

I crutched it into his office, prepared for the worst and found my attorney Bruno standing there.

"Pack your bags, kid!" he said. "You're coming home with me!"

Overjoyed, I dropped my crutches and jumped into his arms.

"All right, all right," he said. "Go grab whatever you need."

I hobbled up to my unit as fast as I could and changed into my civilian clothing. There wasn't much else to bring.

Bruno met me outside of the warden's office and we went out the front door together. It was a bright, beautiful sunny day. Bruno helped me into his Mercedes Benz. We drove off with the windows down and the wind in our hair.

"What's going on?" I asked him. "Did you win the appeal?"

"No, this release is just for graduation."

Bruno saw my disappointment and reached over to place his hand on my arm.

"Hey, we'll win that appeal, but come on. Keep your chin up. I've spent all kinds of time getting you out for a couple of days. Let's enjoy this."

"Okay. So how did it all happen?"

"Well, first of all, let me tell you. There's this Judge Hoffman. He's one of the superior court judges who heard your appeal. Man oh man, he makes old Murkowski seem like a Boy Scout."

I smiled as I listened and nodded.

"Yeah, that bad," Bruno said. "Anyway, I had to make a trip down to superior court. With it being close to three hours each way, it was no picnic. We met in his private chambers. I handed him my request. He looked at it like I was a biker asking to marry his daughter. He told me, 'I've never issued a document of this sort in my entire twenty years of experience.' I told him, 'Well I guess this is going to be your first time.'"

"So, it worked?"

"No, not immediately. I was instructed to meet with a review panel. After I met with the three judges on the panel, one of the judges asked me to wait outside."

Bruno looked over at me with a smile.

"That was unusual. That had never happened to me before in all my years of practice. So I went out and sat, twiddling my thumbs. Ten minutes later, a clerk came out, asked when the graduation day was and disappeared back inside. A few moments after that, the clerk reappeared with the release."

Bruno gave me another smile.

"I let out a huge sigh of relief and immediately called the director of the juvenile probation department from a pay phone. I was extremely pleased about picking you up for graduation but this director lady wasn't particularly happy about the idea. I know you never met her but take my word, the woman is not kind. She's all about more jails and throwing everybody behind bars. She gave me all kinds of grief about how it was after hours when I called. Anyway, I have to drive over to her place after I drop you off to show her the official copy. It'll be worth the drive just to see the lousy look on her face."

Just then, we passed a fast-food place and I asked Bruno if we could stop.

"I haven't had a cheeseburger and fries for almost a month."

Bruno laughed out loud and quickly pulled off.

It was mid-afternoon when we pulled up in front of Bruno's office. My parents came rushing out to the car.

"Oh, my goodness," my mother said. "It is so good to have you home."

There were tears and hugs all around and then we went inside to talk a little. Bruno put his hand on my father's shoulder.

"I've already explained everything to Justin."

Dad looked at me.

"Are you all right with that, Justin?"

"Yeah, I just wish it could be longer."

"Oh, all right," Mom said. "So let's just enjoy the time we have together. Okay? Besides, Maria is dying to see you."

That thought made me smile and I immediately called her.

"Can you meet us at my place? We should be there in twenty or thirty minutes."

She agreed and came up the driveway a short time after we had arrived back. I went racing out on my crutches to greet her. The crutches were dropped as we embraced. My mother discreetly closed the door to the house.

After visiting with my family for a while, Maria asked if it was all right for us to go hang out at her place.

"Just make sure you have him back here by nine," my mother said. "He's still officially on probation."

"Of course," Maria said.

We hurried out to her car and left.

At the base of the driveway, Maria pulled over so we could kiss again. At one point we stopped and looked into each other's eyes. Maria stroked my hair and face tenderly.

"It feels so perfect to be with you," I said. "I don't ever want to go back again."

"Shhh," Maria said and kissed my face. We held each other close and my stress disappeared.

"Let's get out of here," I said.

"Okay," Maria said.

On the way to Maria's house, she asked me what it was like being locked up in juvenile hall and I explained everything that had happened to me from the Greenville Detention Center to St. Jude's. When I told her about Sean and his Vanilla Ice impression, she laughed.

At Maria's place, she helped me out with the crutches and hurried up the sidewalk in front of me. The minute I poked my head inside the front door, I heard a chorus of voices say, "Surprise!"

Maria's family was there with funny hats on. A bunch of party favors popped and filled the air with streamers.

"Hey, Justin, it's great to see you," Ellen said. "Come on in. We're going to have a nice little party for you."

Everyone in the family gave me a hug and said how happy they were to see me. I had to laugh seeing Nick with that funny hat on and blowing into the noisemaker.

Maria led me to the kitchen, where a big banner had been strung from the ceiling that read, WELCOME HOME. There was a cake on the counter with the same sentiment written across the top.

Over dinner, I related some of the stories I had already shared with Maria. I told them about Darnell, Jamal and Stan, and the great compassion I had for these unfortunate guys who came from broken homes. They were always sitting up late at night, laughing and talking, but behind the laughter, it was impossible to forget how much harder their lives had been than mine.

After the cake and ice cream plates were put away, Ellen turned down the lights in the kitchen.

"Time for you to go to bed," she said to the kids.

They went off whining. Ellen smiled at us.

"I'm sure you two want to be left alone. Nick and I will be watching a movie out in the living room if you need us."

"Thanks, Mom," Maria said and we went to her room. Making up for lost time, we made the most of the little time we would have together. We laughed, we talked, and we enjoyed intimate moments.

Maria got me home just before nine, but we sat out in the driveway for another hour, kissing and talking. Finally I went into the house to sleep, my mind savoring the beautiful evening with Maria and her family but also nervous and excited about the graduation ceremony at school. There had only been a brief window between the yearbook episode and the time I was led off to juvenile prison and the wretched feelings of that day were still vivid in my mind. I could almost visualize the looks on my classmates' faces.

I woke up the next morning filled with anxiety. My parents and I sat around the table, having breakfast and talking about life in general. Any conversation having to do with Dickie and prisons was not even brought up.

After breakfast, Mom drove me over to school. She turned on the radio along the way. A song had just concluded and the announcer came on.

"Hey, I just heard the Hellerman shooter is home for graduation. I think that's great. Why don't you call in and tell us how you feel about it?"

My mother quickly changed the channel. I look straight ahead, shocked and taken off my guard. My mother shook my arm.

"Hey, don't worry, honey. Everything will be fine."

I nodded, but the controversial nature of my attendance for graduation was becoming all too clear to me. Of course some folks would be happy to see me, but I'm sure that some would not.

My mother pulled into the school parking lot and stopped directly in front of the main entrance. She gave me a big hug and a kiss as I prepared to get out.

"Do you know how much I love you?" she asked.

"I know Mom. I love you, too."

"Keep your chin up," she said with an adoring look.

I took a deep breath, put on a smile and got out of the car.

Once again I placed the crutches under my arms and hobbled in. She drove off as I entered the building. Today was only the commencement practice. Tomorrow would be the actual graduation, but everyone was there and I was incredibly nervous. I could hardly breathe as I entered the school. The principal was there, greeting kids at the door.

"Hey, Justin!" he said upon seeing me. "We're so glad you're here. Listen, I need for you to come by my office for a bit, all right? Before we head over to the commencement practice?"

"Sure," I said, unsure of what he wanted, but not expecting it was anything good.

As I settled into a chair in his office, we heard screaming out in the hallway. The principal excused himself and went back outside. I quickly realized it was Roy Hellerman hollering.

"This kid kills my son and now he's out of jail for graduation! Where's the justice in that? My son's in a grave right now because of that kid!"

Eventually, I heard the commotion die down and the principal came back in.

"Sorry," he said, sitting down. "I hope you didn't hear that. Are you all right?"

"Oh yeah, I'm fine."

Knowing Roy was there and hearing his hateful words had brought back all my old fears, but I pretended I was unfazed.

"I'll tell you what. Let's head over to the gymnasium and let your fellow classmates know you're here. I don't know how the word got out. We purposefully kept things quiet about your being here for graduation, but I still think it's a big surprise for most everyone."

I felt the same fears as we made our way over to the gym. How would my classmates respond to seeing me?

The principal opened the door and we walked in with everyone's back facing us. The vice principal was giving a speech up front and acknowledged my arrival with a smile and a thumbs up.

"Hey everyone," he announced. "I have a big surprise for you. Justin Bailey just walked in and he's here to attend the graduation with us."

Everyone either stood up in a rush or turned their heads to look at me. I waited with dread. Then all of a sudden I had a rush of well-wishers around, greeting me.

I lost it and began to cry. One after another, my fellow classmates came over and welcomed me back. There were one or two who looked on with hateful stares, but most everyone came up to offer their understanding and acceptance.

Late that night I lay alone in bed, aware that anonymous threats had been called in to the school, forcing school officials to hold the ceremony inside. Everyone was on alert and they were taking no chances. If someone from the Hellerman clan showed up to make a big scene, they would be ready.

The graduation ceremony was planned for early afternoon the next day. My mom took me to the school around noon.

"Your dad and I will be back in a little bit," she said. "I love you. See you soon."

"I love you too, Mom."

As I entered the school, I looked back and saw her still watching me. Only when I was safely inside did she drive away.

When I went into the office to pick up my cap and gown, one of the secretaries quickly ran off to retrieve the principal. As I was heading back out, he appeared.

"Justin, please come with me. I need to go over a few things with you prior to the graduation ceremony."

Out in the hallway, we turned the corner toward his office and were met by two police officers. Immediately I had a sick feeling in my stomach. Why did my life have to be so complicated?

"Sorry, Justin, but these officers are here for your protection. They will be close by in case anything comes up today."

I nodded my head in acknowledgement.

"Hey Justin," the principal said as I was turning away. I turned back to him.

"Sorry again, but it has to be this way."

Again I nodded. I did understand but was both agitated and embarrassed about everything. I just wanted to fit in as best as I could. Instead I had a police escort.

There was about an hour to waste before graduation so I made my way over to the cafeteria. All of my classmates were gathered around, trying to figure out the etiquette of their caps and gowns and talking.

"Do you wear it with the tassel on the left or the right?"

"How long is this thing going to last. We need to get started on partying."

"Hey, check it out. I'm only wearing my boxer shorts under this."

One kid had flashed a group of us. The jokes went on and on.

After a spell, a couple of my friends and I decided to walk the grounds of the school for old time's sake. The police officers were kind enough to keep a distance. A camera crew for the yearbook came along and took a photo of me and my two buddies. I was in the middle with two of my behemoth buddies, Ethan and Charlie, holding my crutches.

We heard a buzz among our fellow students and realized it was time to head back to the gymnasium. The ceremony was about to start. The place had turned into a zoo in our absence. Besides the throng of family and friends filling the stands, there was a crush of news media up near the stage. The big TV stations, the local newspapers, all of them had come out to capture a convicted killer celebrating his graduation day.

A staff of teachers and volunteers were outside the doors, helping to organize the students. I looked in again and saw the media poised to begin. Then one of the teachers flung open the gym doors. The graduation music of "Pomp and Circumstance" began and one by one the students began to file in, the graduation march had begun. Family and friends were snapping pictures as their loved ones appeared. The scene was magical at times.

We were arranged in order by our last names, so I was one of the first to go in. The reporters started snapping pictures like crazy as I entered on my crutches. I kept my head down and hurriedly took my seat.

After some pageantry, several long speeches, and a few words from the superintendent, the first row of students made their way up to the stage to receive their diplomas. When it was time for my row to stand up, the camera flashes of the media really lit up in front of the gymnasium. As I swung my way across the stage on my crutches, the light show was perpetual.

"Congratulations, Justin," the superintendent said, in handing me my diploma. I fumbled with my crutches and shook his hand as I thanked him.

I returned to my seat in another burst of camera flashes. A couple of my classmates stuck their tongues out at the cameramen in protest and booed. I found that to be comical and giggled to myself.

Once all the diplomas had been distributed, there were more speeches. Students sat joking and squirming. Then at last it was time to throw our caps in the air.

A more or less orderly procession of students filed outside, where we were greeted by family and friends. My parents and Maria's entire family greeted me as I came out. With great happiness, all the graduates ran about congratulating each other and posing for the endless combinations of family/graduate photos with grandmas, siblings, friends, and parents.

As I stood near the door to the gymnasium with my family, the parents of one of the students came up to greet me.

"Great job, Justin," the father said. "We're really glad you were here today."

Another family came up, then another.

"Congratulations, Justin, welcome home."

"We're so glad you braved the media attention."

To my amazement, it appeared that nearly every single person inside of that gymnasium came up to offer their words of support. With each new hug, I broke down in tears, overwhelmed by one of the simple rites of passage of my young life.

Eventually everyone was finished saying goodbye and was wandering off. With a last few words of love and support, I was left standing there with Maria and my parents. My eyes were red from crying. My father passed me some tissues and I blew my nose. It suddenly sank in as I dried my tears. My freedom was just about over. Everyone else was headed off to graduation parties, just like I had been a year ago. But I was now a convicted killer, on my way back to juvenile prison. I broke down and wept again, even as my mother was arranging for Maria to have dinner with us before I left.

Defending My Life

Seventeen

The ride back home was mostly a quiet one. The images of graduation day played over and over in my mind. On the one extreme was the heartwarming way in which my classmates and their families had supported me. On the other was the way the media had turned the event into a circus for everyone. Then I remembered again that my brief freedom was about to end.

Maria felt me squeezing her hand tightly and looked over my way. She smiled as I looked out at the passing country.

After a quiet dinner, Maria and I spent a few hours walking back up to the big rock and talking along the way. I was due back at St. Jude's early in the morning so she got up to leave around nine. I walked her out to the car.

"Will you come see me?" I asked after a spell.

"Sure. You know I will."

"Holy crap, I'm going to be locked up in that place until I'm twenty-one years old."

I was sad and she comforted me.

"I'll come see you," she said. "Just let me know as soon as you have some visitation rights."

She climbed in the car and we kissed through the open window.

"I guess you could write me in the meantime," I hinted broadly.

"Yeah, I'll write to you, okay? Goodbye, I love you."

We kissed one more time before she drove away. I stood and watched her go. At the door to the house, my mother took me in her arms and tried to assure me that everything would be all right.

"You just have to get through the next stretch," she said and pulled back to look at me. "You've got a whole long life ahead of you."

"Every time I think of that, I realize how Dickie doesn't." It was a constant realization that I carried with me always.

"Oh, Justin," she said.

She held me again until my grief had subsided and we walked back inside the house.

I lay awake for a while, dwelling on how my friends were probably out having a great time and I wasn't. It felt like a knife in my heart. I was being punished for defending my life. Where was the fairness in that?

I awoke in the morning feeling as if I had not slept a bit. No one said much during breakfast and then we were on our way back to St. Jude's. I slept most of the way there. It was very quiet in the front seat and I noticed my parents glancing back at me from time to time.

After a few hours, I felt my mother gently shaking me.

"Honey, wake up."

I sat up to find that we had arrived. I was instantly depressed by the sight of the building.

When we got out of the car, both of my parents hugged me.

"I guess it's best if we say goodbye out here," Mom said. She looked to my father. "We won't have much privacy in there."

She began to cry and hugged me. My father joined in.

"Pull yourself together, Justin," he said. "Be strong, for me."

"Okay dad. Goodbye. I love you."

"I love you, too."

Inside, the attendant quickly took me from my parents to be processed. There was a final wave before Mike escorted me back up to Beta block. We walked slowly, with Mike seeming to understand the stress of my situation. First locked up, then gloriously freed for just a few days, I was being re-introduced to my dreadful life of loneliness, boredom, and being treated like one of society's pariahs.

"How did that graduation go?" he asked.

"Okay," I said.

He looked over at me.

"I know, I know. It's hard to come back. But at least you had the chance to go."

"Yeah," I muttered.

As we walked, I told him about the media frenzy and Roy showing up to protest.

"Yeah, that sounds rough," he said. "That sounds really rough, but I take it you're okay now, right?"

I shrugged, not having a cheerful answer.

We came to my block and Mike patted me on the back.

"Good to see you again, kid. Even though I know you're not glad to see us."

Mike trudged off in his world-weary way. I don't think he wanted to see anyone inside of St. Jude's, but especially not me.

After I had checked in at Beta block, I was allowed to join the others out in the yard. The usual activity was in full swing, guys gathered around in gangs, smoking cigarettes and watching the basketball games being played by other inmates. The games were exciting.

I noticed a new guy hanging out with Darnell and Stanley. He was a little under six feet and easily weighed about 300 pounds.

He was playing the part of a tough guy – tattoos all over his arms and neck, talking smack, but I saw right through him. He didn't have the edge of Jamal. Take away 150 pounds and he was nothing but a big kid.

"Hey, look here," Stan said, seeing me come out the door. "It's our honky with the weekend pass."

I swung over on my crutches.

"Careful with this boy," Stanley told the new guy. "He capped a dude, and if he don't like you, he's gonna cap you, too."

Omar stared at me. I adjusted my crutches and held out my hand.

"Justin."

"Omar."

"You really cap someone?"

I nodded. "It's not something I'm proud of."

Omar nodded back with respect.

"Well, you'd better use a .45 on me. I don't go down easy."

"Well hopefully it doesn't come to that."

Omar stared. Stanley started laughing. Finally Omar smiled.

"You're pretty damned serious for a honky who just got a vacation."

"This guy keeps telling us he's from Guatemala but I know he's just another beaner."

"Screw you, Stanley."

"No habla Espanol?"

Omar went after Stanley in fun.

"Hey, Justin," Stanley said, coming back. "Did you get any action while you were out there?"

I sat down.

"There wasn't enough time, man."

"Aw don't gimme that! You've got to be kiddin' me. Ain't no time? Damn, two minutes would have been enough time."

"You're a real romantic, Stanley," I said.

"Man, there's nothin' more romantic than that, baby."

He and Darnell had a big laugh motioning the positions they would have used.

"So, what else happened out there, man? Tell us all about it."

I did, including the part about Roy Hellerman and the media frenzy.

"You hear that, Darnell? If I shoot someone's ass, I'm gonna be famous. All I did was steal a couple of cars and sell some weed. I don't see anyone taking my picture."

Seeing me looking glum, Stanley patted me on the back.

"It's all right, Justin. I'd have shot that sucker's ass too."

I nodded.

"But you should have gotten some nookie."

"I told you, there wasn't time and believe me, I wanted to."

Just then Jamal had an awesome slam dunk and a great ruckus broke out among the two teams. Some were cheering. Some were booing. Amazingly, these battles on the court never led to a riot.

"What the hell happened to Vanilla Ice, anyway?"

"Oh, that boy's in trouble with everyone now. Thinks he's a real thug rapper. Oh look, here he comes."

Sean came over acting like some sort of tough guy. He was all bruised up with scabs on his chin.

"Hey," Stan said. "Show us some break dancing, man."

"Back off, bro, I ain't taking any more of your crap."

Sean went off, talking to himself.

"They're gonna haul him off in a straight jacket one of these days soon," Darnell said.

"I'll give him about a week," Stan said.

They laughed. I watched Sean walk off, almost feeling sorry for him.

When it was time for lunch, everyone lined up and filed back up to the second floor. After lunch, it was time to hang around Beta block. The staff offered no structure. A lot of the kids watched TV. Some played cards. I used the opportunity to write Maria a letter.

Dinner was served at the same time every day, followed by more chill time on Beta block, our last, late walk down in the yard, a shower, bed, then up early to start all over again.

The next day was laundry day but St. Jude's had no washers or dryers. Everything had to be done by hand in a five-gallon bucket. I filled mine with cold water, detergent and used one of my crutches to churn the dirty clothes around. It was one hell of a chore. A minute or two and my muscles were burning.

The guards provided us with some twine to hang our clothes out to dry. The whole event was animated by comical stories. Guys bragged about stealing cars and selling drugs. Mostly they talked about all the chicks they knew, what fine cars they were going to have and what they would do when they got out.

"Man, I hate this place. It really sucks. I can't wait to get out of here."

I heard that a lot. Then it was back to Beta block and time for lunch.

Mike came up to our block after lunch. He gave me a pat on the back.

"How are you doing, Justin?"

"Okay. I was hoping I never had to come back though."

"Yeah, you'll be going home soon enough. I've got a feeling."

He got Darnell and Stanley's attention and waved them over.

"Good news for you guys. All of you are going to the amusement park this weekend."

"Man, that is all right," Darnell said, parading around.

Mike quieted him and the rest of us.

"Look, we don't want to rub it in anyone's nose."

Darnell and Stanley huddled in close.

"So, what's up, Big Mike?"

"Well, first thing, Stanley, I need you to go find Jamal and Omar. They're coming, too."

Stanley went off. Mike sat down with Darnell and me.

"Now, here's the thing, you two. If you want to meet with your family, or in your case, Justin, with your sweetheart, then you need to give them a call and set things up. I'm fine with it as long as we all get back in one piece."

Darnell and I high-fived each other without saying a word. Stanley came back with Jamal, Omar and Mike quickly explained the rules to them. There were more high-fives. We struggled to contain ourselves all day.

When I called my folks, they said they couldn't make it. My father would have needed more time to arrange a day off from work, but Maria said she would definitely come. Ditto for her folks and the kids.

For three more days we hid our anticipation. Then we were finally down in front of the building, climbing into a big white passenger van with Mike as the driver. There was lots of joking. The big argument was trying to figure out who would wimp out of the scariest rides.

Maria and her family were waiting for me in front when we arrived. Everyone gathered around and Mike explained the rules for the day. Check in back at the gate every hour and be ready to leave at six in the evening. Everyone went their separate ways.

It was a cool summer day, cloudy and breezy. Maria and I got everyone to agree on the roller coaster first. The line was long but Maria and I were just happy to be together, holding hands, hugging each other and talking.

After a few roller coaster rides, we decided to have lunch. Nick handed me the keys to their van. They brought all kinds of food and beverages and they were in the van.

"Hey, hon," he said to Ellen. "Why don't we go shopping down on Main Street."

"Sure," Ellen said with a smile. "We'll plan to meet back here in say, an hour?"

"Sure, mom," Maria said.

We started off.

"Hey," Ellen called after us. She looked at her watch. "Don't forget to check in with Mike, Justin. It's about that time."

I gave her a thumbs up and headed over the main gate. Mike was waiting there. We had beaten everyone else back.

"Hey, Justin, Maria. You two having lots of fun?"

"Yeah Mike, everything's great."

"Well, go on. No need for you to hang around waiting for the others. I'll see you back here in another hour."

"Thanks, Mike."

Maria and I made sure Mike was looking the other way before we hurried out to the parking lot. Nick had already pulled all the curtains shut in the van. Maria and I rolled down some of the windows part way to let in the breeze.

"Your folks are so cool," I said.

"Yeah, they are, but come on. It's not like we're kids anymore. I'm in college."

"Yeah," I said. "Sometimes I forget we're growing up."

I was sitting on one of the back seats. Maria came over and sat on my lap, facing me.

"Did you miss me?"

"Yeah."

Then we proceeded to show each other just how much we

had missed each other. When we stopped to catch our breath, we held each other tightly.

"Oh, baby. I love you," whispered Maria.

"I love you, too."

"I wish we didn't have to be apart."

"Please don't talk about it. I'm trying to do as Dr. Delano told me. Stay in the moment. When I do that, I'm okay. If I start thinking ahead, even to tomorrow, I go crazy."

After eating a sandwich, we sipped on some ice water from the cooler. Noticing that time was passing quickly, we hurried back to meet her family.

At the end of the day, we met up with Mike and the other guys. There was laughter and tearful goodbyes. I wasn't sad as much as I was grateful. It had been a wonderful day and someday I would have my freedom back to live life the way I wanted.

I hugged Maria and everyone else in her family and climbed into the St. Jude's van.

On the way back, everyone talked about what they had done.

"I'll bet you Stanley screamed like a girl on the roller coaster rides," I said.

"Screw you," Stanley said. "I just want to know if you got some. "Cuz if you didn't, I'm gonna be real disappointed."

"Well, I guess you're going to have to be disappointed."

"Oh man, you honkies. Don't even know how to get some action."

I smiled to myself, happy to keep my intimate experiences private.

I drifted off to sleep and woke up as we pulled to a stop out in front of the building. It was dark. We all made our way upstairs in silence, tired but grateful. No one had to tell us to keep this day to ourselves.

"Thanks," I said to Mike before he left.

"That's all right, Justin. You just work hard on making next month's list, so we can go see that ballgame."

I went to sleep thinking about that, and remembering Maria in my arms.

Eighteen

The days turned to weeks and the weeks into another month. Stanley, Darnell, Omar, Jamal and I continued to bond together. We took smoke breaks with the other people in our group. Somehow we always got back to talking about the shooting. There was never any shortage of questions. In the end, these were just kids, lost kids, naïve kids and never as big as their talk. To them, I was some kind of bad-ass dude for doing what I did. The fact was, if they had shot someone, they'd likely be doing hard time in the big boy jail. Maybe they already had. They weren't exactly forthcoming with the details of their personal mischief.

Either way, having killed someone got me a lot of respect. Being on crutches got me that much more slack.

One day, Sean came over to me in the yard. His face was littered with more bruises and cuts. He was scurrying around on the ground. It looked like he had totally lost it.

"Dude, what the hell are you doing?" I asked him.

"Looking for old cigarette butts, bro. You get enough of these and you can roll your own smoke."

He opened his palm as if he was holding several cigarette butts. There was a mad look on his face. I realized the guy had crossed over the line and moved a safe distance away from him with my crutches.

A few minutes later, the guards caught wind of Sean and off he went, one guard on either side of him, his feet hardly touching the ground.

Stan came back from a visit a short while later.

"What did you do to your boy?" he asked me.

"Nothing."

"You must have done something, they just took him away in a straight jacket."

"You're friggin' kidding me."

"I'm not kidding you, bro. Just like we were saying that night. What the hell did he do?"

"He was out here pretending to pick up cigarette butts off the ground."

"What!" Stan said in disbelief.

"I ain't making this up, man. He was rolling and smoking them, too."

"This place is gonna drive all of us friggin' crazy."

He went off, shaking his head.

"That poor old knuckleheaded cracker. I guess maybe we rode him too hard."

One day bled into another. It was the same routine, day after day. We'd get a wakeup call, file in to have breakfast, file out to the yard, file back in for lunch, then dinner, file off for our final warm-down out in the yard, showers, off to bed and back up for breakfast again.

The meals came along on an assembly line and you picked out whatever entree you wanted. There were no snacks in between so you ate up or found yourself hungry.

The guards were a pain in the ass for the most part and treated us like we were hardcore criminals. Talking was discouraged and they made us sit with different people at meals every day. I guess they figured it would hold the gang stuff to a minimum or something.

"All right, get your meals and sit the hell down."

"Less talking and more eating."

We heard that stuff a lot.

"Finish up, girls, it's time to go."

"What do you think? You on vacation here?"

I never did get used to the lack of trust. There was always suspicion coming down from above, plus arrogance and antagonism. You weren't supposed to make a move unless you were ordered to do so or had received permission.

"Step to it, get in line!"

I went along without trouble. Stanley wasn't so cooperative. I'd hear him singinging under his voice behind me.

"Swing low, Sweet chariot…"

"You got something to say?" the guard said back.

"No, I got nothin', boss. Just shakin' the bush."

"All right, just keep the sarcasm to yourself."

"Yes sir, mister boss, sir."

Everyone was silently cracking up with the guards not finding any of it to be funny.

After a while, I was issued a visitation privilege and my mother and Maria showed up to visit me. As usual, my father was unable to come because of his work, but I was used to that.

We engaged in small talk for the most part. I asked about my brothers and how things were going around town. I brought up the subject of my appeal but my mother said that she hadn't heard anything new lately. The rest of the visit was sort of depressing after that. I felt no peace and we had no privacy. There was too little time to really enjoy their company as happy as I was to see them.

That visit had coincided with my lunch hour so Mom and Maria joined me in the cafeteria. We made our way through the line with other inmates talking around us. They made some effort to keep the usual rap down to a minimum, but I could feel Maria's and my mother's discomfort as the guards walked around keeping the peace.

I was more embarrassed by the quality of the food. This wasn't home-cooking by a long stretch. Things were just sort of slopped onto your plate.

Before I knew it, the visit was over. I walked them out to the gate. It was depressing to say goodbye. I went back inside in a funk.

Stanley and Darnell saw that I was down and invited me for a smoke break.

"Cheer up, gimpy," Stanley said as a joke.

"I'm just down, man. It's a bummer not being able to leave with them."

"Do you think we feel any different, you dumb cracker?" Darnell asked.

"Did you get any?" Stan asked. "That's what I want to know?"

Stanley and Darnell were all smiles, high-fiving each other. I had to smile watching them. It was a great mood changer.

"Well?" Stanley asked, when he was done high-fiving.

"No way, dude. My mother was right there. Anyway, how the hell are you supposed to get anything in the chow hall?"

"If my girl was here, she woulda given it up."

He went strutting around with a smile and we laughed at him.

"Right!" I said. "Stanley, the babe hound."

"Hey, next time she comes around, you just let me know and I'll show you how to get it done."

Stanley kept parading around, with everyone laughing at him.

The next day I was playing ping-pong with Darnell when Jamal came in and butted into the game.

"I've been wanting to play you," Jamal said to me.

Jamal was well over six feet, solid muscle and imposing. He played like Charles Barkley on the basketball court and nobody messed with him. He had made one bad decision after another and seemed destined to a life behind bars. His attitude didn't help things any, but like most everyone in there, he respected me.

We played a game and I whipped his butt. Even with the cast I was pretty damned good.

"You just got lucky," Jamal said, and challenged me to another game.

I beat him again. Then he was pissed.

Mike came by and intervened.

"You know what? Why don't we have a tournament to see who's the best?"

"Now that's what I'm talkin' about," Jamal said. "I'll be whipping this little honky."

Mike arranged it so that all the guys on Beta block were the tournament. It was a week of intense game play.

In the end, the finals came down to Jamal and I. He was grunting and groaning and stretched halfway across the table with every serve. He'd make loud screams every time he won a point, but I held my own and beat him again.

I razzed Jamal for losing and he razzed me back.

"Ya know I had to let you win because you're a cripple."

"Yeah, right," I said, agreeing and nodding.

Jamal could have beaten me to a pulp, but he had a good soul beneath all that anger at the world. You found yourself rooting for him. You hoped he would get out and find his way. It wasn't meant to be.

Shortly after that ping-pong tournament, Jamal went off on one of the guards again. They sent him away for a while. They never said where, but when he came back, he wasn't the same. He had retreated inside himself somewhere. Society had branded him a bad guy and those wounds seemed to have covered over every kindness that was left in him. Then one day he started a fight out in the yard over a basketball game. The last I saw of Jamal he was being torn off the other kid. It was a pretty bad beating. They cuffed Jamal and hauled him off to do hard time, I think. I never got to see him again or say goodbye.

They took Darnell away a few weeks later. Being away from his little girl finally got to him and he tried to escape. It was his third time so they moved him to a maximum security lock-up somewhere else. His bed was empty for a while before a new kid moved in. Things were never the same after that.

I began to lose track of time. It was a good thing in a way. The days and weeks just seemed to slip on by. The daily cycle was a never-ending loop. You didn't expect many highs. You hoped there weren't too many lows. There was nothing much to look forward to except winning the monthly contest.

We did and Mike arranged to take a bunch of us to a major league baseball game, as promised.

Three days before the game, they finally took my cast off and replaced it with an air cast that I was able to take off at will. I was still hobbling around a bit but my mobility had been increased tenfold.

We took off on a Sunday morning in the warmth of summer. Mike had a big grin on his face the entire way there. When we got to the stadium, we chattered on in excitement the whole way to our seats.

The two teams traded runs until the bottom of the final inning and the home team eked out a win. The crowd went wild and we all had a blast. It took us most of an hour to get out of the stadium and back on the road.

We were talking about the game all the way home. We were all baseball fans and found camaraderie in our love for the game that day. One day of fun per month did not make up for twenty-nine days of drudgery, but even that one day of semi-freedom was relief from the mind-numbing tedium of our normal routine.

The next week, it was scorching hot outside so they let everyone go down to the pool to cool off. They usually only allowed us to swim once a week, if that, but when it was sweltering hot, they made an exception.

It was after lunch and I was having a good time watching everyone play. It was remarkable how even the most hardcore inmates acted ten years younger when they were splashing around in a pool. I was especially thrilled because this was the first chance I had had to swim in a long time. I was just climbing out of the pool after another swim when I saw a car that looked like my parents' car driving by.

"Holy crap, that looked like my parents' car," I said to Stanley.

"You must be dreamin'. He's seein' a mirage in this crazy heat," Stan said to the guy next to me.

"No, no, man. I really think it was my parents' car."

Twenty minutes went by, and with every additional minute, Stanley was ramping up the jive.

"Guess your parents went right on by, huh? They don't care about your skinny little behind."

Everyone within earshot was laughing.

Then Mike stuck his head out into the yard.

"Justin, come on over here, I need to talk to you."

"Must be the president come to see you, cracker."

I slipped on the walking boot for my ankle and hurried off with everyone calling out and laughing at me. One of the kids followed me over to the door.

"Justin, your parents are here."

"Hey, Stanley," the kid called out. "He wasn't lying. His parents are here."

Stanley and a bunch of other kids started crowding around.

"Come on," Mike said with a big smile. "It's time for you to go."

"What do you mean? What's going on?"

"Your parents are here to take you home."

I stood there, not knowing what to do.

"Well don't just stand there staring like a dummy," Stanley said. "Get the heck out of here."

"I don't understand. What's going on?"

My mind was racing.

"Your appeal went through, Justin. You're going home for good."

I stood there in disbelief, my eyes welling up with tears. I turned to Stanley.

"I'm going home, man."

"Hey!" he said out loud. "This boy is going home!"

"Shh," Mike said. "Don't be telling everybody he's getting out when they can't. He might catch all kinds of trouble from the others."

But by then several members of my block were already chanting.

"Justin's going home!"

Stanley and some of the other guys hoisted me up on their shoulders and paraded me around like I had won the state championship.

"Justin's going home! Justin's going home!"

They kept chanting.

I looked over and saw the happiness in Mike's eyes. I was happy, too. I couldn't believe these guys were so genuinely glad for me, when they were still stuck in this place.

A few minutes later, as Mike and I arrived out to the processing area, I saw my parents and Maria waiting on the other side of the gate. They stood up from their chairs, eager with anticipation but had to wait patiently another twenty minutes before I was free to go through the door to be with them.

We embraced in tears. I saw Mike over Maria's shoulder. He smiled and disappeared back into the prison and I never saw him again.

Mike was a great man. He always treated me like a human being and not a criminal.

"Let's go home," my father said.

We went outside into a sunny day. My nightmare was over. The next chapter of my life was about to begin.

Epilogue

My life did begin anew as a result of my taking someone's life. Every single day for over twenty years, the memory of that tragic incident has replayed in my mind. It is said that time heals all wounds, but that old adage is hollow consolation for me. The valid fact that I acted in self-defense does not change the reality that I ended someone's life. That person's family is forever changed due to the loss they experienced.

It had been suggested to me in the past that I could live a long, happy life and that some day it would seem much more bearable to me. The reality is that it would take me more than ten years to come to terms with the guilt and depression that I felt for killing someone. Over those years I was constantly looking for outlets to escape my mental trauma, turning with regularity to drugs and alcohol. I doubt that I will ever forget those last two years of high school or the devastation that rained upon every person involved. One could say that, in a way, Dickie continued to bully me for many years even after his death. Dickie lost his life and I lost my ability to control mine.

I recall thinking in those days, months and years following the shooting, why is this happening to me? Isn't life difficult enough without this horrible burden? Other people seem to live a much more carefree existence. Why me?

I guess the truth is that we all struggle with different challenges throughout life, whether they are self-induced, are brought on by others, or are natural occurrences. The best advice I ever received was that you need to face life's challenges head-on and not let them run your life. In other words, you can take the difficulties that you are handed in life and let them consume you or you can come to terms with it and move on. It took me a long time to heed that advice.

We hear much about the dangers and ill effects of bullying in today's news. I was a victim of another's bullying and the result of that particular episode was ultimately disastrous to both of us and our families. My hope is that this story may serve as caution to those who would harm others physically, verbally or in any other way and for communities and schools to be ever vigilant in watching for signs of such behavior. The damage caused by bullying may be subtle or overwhelming, immediate or delayed, with long-term and completely unpredictable results.

CPSIA information can be obtained at www.ICGtesting.com
Printed in the USA
BVOW011017281112

306724BV00002B/37/P